John Bonham
A THUNDER OF DRUMS

Backbeat
Books

John Bonham

A THUNDER OF DRUMS

THE POWERHOUSE

BEHIND LED ZEPPELIN

AND THE GODFATHER

OF HEAVY

ROCK DRUMMING

Chris Welch and Geoff Nicholls

Backbeat Books

John Bonham
A THUNDER OF DRUMS

Chris Welch and Geoff Nicholls

A BACKBEAT BOOK
First edition 2001

Published by Backbeat Books
600 Harrison Street,
San Francisco, CA 94107
www.backbeatbooks.com

An imprint of The Music Player Network
United Entertainment Media, Inc.

Produced for Backbeat Books by Outline Press Ltd,
115J Cleveland Street,
London W1T 6PU, England.
www.balafon.dircon.co.uk

ISBN 0-87930-658-0

Art Director: Nigel Osborne
Design: Sally Stockwell
Editors: Paul Quinn, Tony Bacon

Origination by Global Colour (Malaysia)
Printed in Singapore by Tien Wah Press

01 02 03 04 05 5 4 3 2 1

CONTENTS

A THUNDER OF DRUMS

John was the greatest drummer
in the world. I knew that because he
told me so.

ROBERT PLANT

John Bonham was one of the most influential rock drummers of all time. A founder member of Led Zeppelin, hailed by a generation of fans and critics as one of the world's greatest bands, Bonham's exploits away from the drums have attained mythical status – but it was his achievements as an innovative and individual musician that ensure his lasting fame.

John 'Bonzo' Bonham provided the energy that galvanised Led Zeppelin into action when they burst on the scene back in 1968. The sheer audacity of his drumming was a perfect match for the electrifying guitar of Jimmy Page and Robert Plant's dynamic vocals. Together with his bass-playing partner John Paul Jones, Bonzo laid down Zeppelin's rhythmic bedrock with unrivalled authority.

The celebrated Bonham sound – a deep, rumbling roar that almost seemed to emanate from the bowels of the earth – was an integral part of such magnificent anthems as 'Kashmir', 'Black Dog', 'Achilles Last Stand' and the brooding 'When The Levee Breaks'.

It was the inspiration for hordes of young drummers, who spent years trying to emulate Bonham's entire approach. Indeed his sound and rhythms were imitated, sampled and synthesised to such an extent that they became the template for most recorded pop music during the later part of the 20th century. Yet John did it all with a pair of sticks, a dazzling right foot, and his bare hands.

Bonham was much more than a loud and bombastic rocker. His unerring sense of timing and his feel for syncopation and swing gave Led Zeppelin a solid sense of purpose, unity and cohesion. While his drumming was rooted in rock'n'roll and he was never shy about playing at full volume, Bonzo understood dynamics. He knew how to listen and when not to play. He was the master of the grand entrance, typified by his performances on Zeppelin classics like 'Rock And Roll' and 'Stairway To Heaven'.

He was the drummer who dared improvise, free-form style, with his cymbals on the Zeppelin masterwork 'Dazed And Confused'. He could play diminuendo and leave pregnant silences few of his rivals had the wit or imagination to employ. But above all he was the man who gave Led Zeppelin such a powerful kick, cheerfully demolishing all opposition, blowing away any band that had the temerity to share the same stage.

In the great age of stadium rock, it was Bonham who set new standards for drum solos with his nightly showcase performance on 'Moby Dick'. But the surging, exhilarating rhythms he employed on tunes like 'Houses Of The Holy' or 'Trampled Underfoot' revealed the full magnificence of Bonham's percussive art. He was much more than Led Zeppelin's showman. He was its heart and soul.

The John Bonham often described as a rampaging, mixed-up rock'n'roll rebel was not the one recognised by his friends, family and fellow musicians. John certainly lived life to the limits. He could be loud, boisterous, extravagant and demanding. A yeoman from the English Midlands, he would speak his mind and sup his pint of ale. Yet he was also sensitive, kind-hearted, witty and generous. As his younger sister Deborah Bonham says, "He was just a lovely, funny man."

From his childhood, growing up in the town of Redditch, Worcestershire, south of Birmingham, he was always "our John". A builder by trade, he was rough and ready and got into scrapes. Yet he was also endearingly enthusiastic, hard working and hungry for success. He wanted above all to be recognised as the best at his job. Whether that meant building a brick wall or playing the drums, he put all he had into every enterprise. He was a proud, stubborn, independent, self-taught, self-made man.

He was also a man of surprising contrasts. While he may have been Led Zeppelin's biggest hell raiser, Bonzo was at heart a family man who loved being at home. He was prone to stage fright and fear of flying, to the point where lengthy overseas touring became an ordeal, best alleviated by pranks and high living.

Bonzo had established most of his characteristic traits, tastes and attitudes long before he achieved fame with Plant, Page and Jones. His love of speed, volume and excitement was well-known to his mates among the bands he played with during his teenage years. When he joined Led Zeppelin, however, his life was transformed. He could afford all the luxuries he had ever dreamed about, and spent so much on cars he became known as the motor dealer's dream customer. But he was generous too, treating old friends and supporting local charities.

The public loved him too, not only for his spirited drumming but also for his blunt, down-to-earth manner. When he appeared in the movie *The Song Remains The Same* driving a drag-racing car at breathtaking speed, intercut with scenes of him pounding his drums and setting fire to his gong, audiences cheered in the film theatres.

Fame and success brought both rewards and problems. Playing drums for Led Zeppelin was the ultimate gig. He was respected by fellow drummers and idolised by fans. He was also an inspiration to his son Jason and sister Debbie, who both pursued careers in music. But with all the adulation and rewards came stress, strain and sheer physical exhaustion. There were times when he had to be dragged on to yet another flight for yet another tour, which seemed more like an endurance test than a pleasure. Most of the problems he encountered later in life could be attributed to this split between his responsibilities to the Zeppelin machine and a yearning for his life at home, on his farm and with his family.

Bonham was no tortured genius or rock'n'roll mystic. What you saw was what you got. He was a man who drove a horse and cart through pomposity. He was also highly competitive and determined to make his mark. His old friend, the late Cozy Powell, remembered his outrageous antics on the club scene around Birmingham, England in the 1960s. "Bonham's idea of a good night out would be to go and jam with various local bands and demolish the drum kit. He used to really love that. We went out several times and there were a couple of guys he didn't get on with too well. He'd say to me, 'Just watch me tonight. I'm going to totally demolish this drum kit.' Sure enough, he would…"

When John Bonham first met Robert Plant and teamed up with him in The Band Of Joy, the singer was left in no doubt about his capabilities. "John was the greatest drummer in the world. I knew that because he told me so."

These were Bonham's most endearing characteristics – his honesty, sheer cheek and driving energy. As friends said, he had a heart of gold. And he always wanted to be respected as a top drummer. Despite the bluster, despite the stories of rock'n'roll excess, he was very serious indeed about his music, his playing and the band he loved.

There was a kind of breathless urgency about John, a need to get things done and use his time to the best advantage. It was perhaps an attitude ingrained from his background as a builder: keeping a weather eye open, giving things a kick to make 'em work, and being determined to finish the job. At the end of the day came the rewards, a drink with your mates and then home to the wife and kids.

Greatly missed and still the topic of endless debate, John Bonham retains his grip on the imagination of all those who grew to admire the drummer whom one studio engineer described as "unrecordable"... Years later it was Bonzo's greatest pleasure to send that critic a suitable present – a gold Led Zeppelin album inscribed to one John Henry Bonham with a note saying, "Thanks for the advice."

CHRIS WELCH, KENT, ENGLAND, JULY 2001

YOUR TIME IS GONNA COME

CHAPTER 1

I was determined to be a drummer …
I was so keen I would have played for
nothing. In fact I did for a long time.

JOHN BONHAM

John Henry Bonham was born on May 31st 1948 in Redditch, Worcestershire, in the Midlands of England. When he was delivered, after 26 hours of labour, his heartbeat stopped. Although a duty doctor had left, a nurse was able to call another doctor, who managed to revive him. The nurse later said it was "a miracle" that the baby had survived.

John's parents were hard-working and industrious – traits which rubbed off on their son. His father and grandfather were also called John Henry Bonham but everyone called John's father Jack. A carpenter by trade, Jack ran a building company with his father, called JH Bonham & Son. His wife Joan (nee Sargent) ran a local newsagent shop to supplement their income as she raised a family that included John, their younger son Michael and daughter Deborah.

Michael Bonham, usually known as Mick, worked as a builder at first, and later became a disc jockey, while sister Debbie became a successful singer with her own band. The family were very proud of their success in the music business, although both parents had initial doubts about John's future when their first-born began making a great deal of noise around the house.

The Bonhams lived in small house in Hunt End, just on the outskirts of town. Redditch is situated about 10 miles south of Birmingham, and south east of Kidderminster, in an area known as the Black Country. It got its name from the sooty black smoke that billowed from numerous factory chimneys, although there was still a great deal of beautiful countryside to be enjoyed.

John was brought up with the expectation that he would one day enter the family construction business, and settle down to "a proper job". Mick Bonham later recalled: "As kids we went to the building sites, because of our granddad's firm, which dad and our uncle Ernie ran. They seemed like mega-playgrounds and me and John were always messing around there."

Even before he began fooling with timber, bricks and sand, John was drawn to another, more creative hobby. He first showed signs of his interest in percussion at the age of five, when he started drumming on a handy bath salts container, which had strands of wire across the bottom to filter the salts. He also began beating out rhythms on a circular coffee tin with knives and forks, creating a realistic snare drum effect.

He was clearly looking for ways to upgrade his makeshift drum kit. In this primitive search for the 'Bonham sound' he went around the kitchen playing all the pots and pans and driving his mother to distraction. In desperation she bought him a real snare drum when he was ten. Mr Bonham was never keen on all the racket but, like all doting dads, he relented and bought John his first proper kit when he was 15-and-a-half. It wasn't exactly the latest model.

"It was almost prehistoric," recalled John later. "Most of it was rust. But I was determined to be a drummer as soon as I left school. I was so keen I would have played for nothing. In fact I did for a long time. But my parents stuck by me."

BONHAM BROTHERS

John and Mick grew up as typical brothers, playing, fighting and generally having a great time. They might have seemed like rivals, but woe betide anyone else who tried to have a go at them. It was the signal for the Bonhams to join forces. Said Mick: "Me and John were very much alike. We'd get to a certain pitch and it would be like all the fun of the fair. But then somebody would only have to look at you or say something wrong and then I wanted to fight the world. John was very much the same. He would be feeling great and then, all of a sudden, someone would upset him.

"We had our fair share of fights. But all brothers do. One minute you love each other and the next minute you are knocking hell out of each other. I can remember as kids I said something to him and he ripped a page out of my *Eagle* annual. So I stamped on his watch. He went and smashed my watch. So I threw a carving knife at him and it stuck in the door, just as mum and dad were coming in.

"When we worked on the building sites, we often had fisticuffs, and he sacked me more times than he sacked anybody else. When we were at school together, John might have been kicking the hell out of me, but as soon as somebody else came near me, the two of us would have a go back. He'd stick up for me every time."

> "His main aim was ... to blow the other drummer off stage"

The Bonham boys were sent to Wilton House private school, which insisted on the pupils wearing a distinctive school uniform. Mick: "The uniform was brown, white and blue stripes with a cap to match. We used to have to walk past another school at the bottom of our road, called St Stephen's. We went to the posh school and they were slumming it. Of course the kids would shout out, 'Got yer pyjamas on?' Our John would say to me, 'Come on, our kid, let's have a bit of this' – and there'd be ten of them! Either he couldn't count or he'd got bad eyesight, because we used to get a kicking every time. We had to run the gauntlet every night."

But they were golden days, Mick reminisced: "We spent a lot of time in dad's caravan or on the boat, fishing and swimming and having lazy Sundays. It all seemed like a halcyon time." The boys both enjoyed sports in general, and Mick recalled that John was a great fan of cricket, until he had his nose broken by a cricket ball. "He wasn't even playing that day. He was sat on the boundary talking to a girl and they shouted, 'duck!' As he turned round the cricket ball smacked him straight in the face."

At the age of 11 John was sent to Lodge Farm County Secondary School, where he stayed from 1960 to 1964. But his pugnacious attitude did not always endear him to the headmaster. Mick remembered: "When he left school the headmaster said John 'wouldn't even make a good dustman'. But when John died, the headmaster said in the local paper what a tremendous pupil he had been...

"John was a rogue, there's no doubt. He was always getting the cane. The headmaster was also the JP [Justice Of The Peace – local judge/magistrate] of the town, and this guy was the business when it came to discipline. You didn't mess with this bloke. He was six-foot-six and very stern, and he gave kids the cane just for walking out of line.

> "There was nothing and no one who was going to stop John from playing"

"The great thing was, when I started secondary school we'd moved house and so I didn't go to Lodge Farm. I went to another school, called Ridgeway. But then John's old headmaster moved to Ridgeway as well, and as soon as he heard my name, I was called into the office. 'Are you any relation to John Bonham?' And that was it... But I always managed to keep out of the headmaster's way. John was always into everything. He wasn't your A1 pupil. In fact he stood out like a sore thumb. He was playing with local bands when he was 14 and still at school. He was no angel."

Despite the scrapes he got into, John tried hard to please. School friends remember him providing the sound effects for a Christmas pantomime. He even brought his drum kit to play at the side of the stage. Noises-off would remain one of his lifelong specialities.

He did very well at carpentry lessons – not surprisingly, given the Bonham family background. He even helped out with a project to build a school greenhouse. Building, carpentry and drumming remained joint obsessions throughout his early years. When pupils were asked what they wanted to do when they left school, none of them could come up with an answer. But John said, 'I want to be a drummer.'"

He also succumbed to the lure of pop stardom and once cycled 48 miles to see Screaming Lord Sutch, when the singer was trying to become a Member of Parliament on behalf of the Monster Raving Loony Party. He wanted to add Sutch's autograph to his prized collection, but couldn't afford the train fare.

THE PASSION FOR DRUMS

John had already started playing with school groups such as The Avengers, and quite early on began sitting in with other bands. His main aim, though, was not simply to take part in a musical jam session, but always to blow the other drummer off the stage and, if possible, take over his gig. "There was nothing and no one who was going to stop John from playing," recalled his brother Mick with some pride.

Although he grew up in the Beatles-dominated 1960s, John was thrilled when he saw swing-era drummer Gene Krupa in the movies and on TV. As Mick explained: "Gene Krupa was god. John went to the see the film *The Benny Goodman Story* with his dad." This 1956 Hollywood biopic featured Krupa playing tom toms on his theme tune 'Sing, Sing, Sing'. John also liked the scene where Gene played with sticks on boiler-room steam pipes in *Beat The Band*, a 1946 movie often shown on TV (it's said, by the way, that the director used real steam and the band's double bass became unglued and fell apart).

John's father was a big fan of trumpeter Harry James and went to see his big-band play at Birmingham Town Hall. John got them all tickets for the concert, and Mick remembers drummer Sonny Payne bouncing sticks off the skins and catching them behind his back. All this was inspirational stuff and encouraged John to become a showman and not just a backing musician. He mainly taught himself to play drums, just by fanatical dedication and constant practice – but he did take some advice. He was not averse to knocking on the doors of complete strangers if he thought the person could help him. One such adviser was drummer Garry Allcock, who also happened to have an interest in cars, one of John's other great passions.

> "My name's John Bonham, I'm a drummer and I'm potty about cars"

Redditch-born Allcock was a few years older than John and was doing an engineering apprenticeship at the Austin Motor Company. When John first met him in 1962, Garry was living in a village outside Redditch – he had recently got married and bought a house in Church Road, two miles away from John's parents' home. Allcock had started playing drums in 1951 and was very much into big-bands and jazz. "I had been playing with orchestras for some years. John was working on a building site at the time – he was obviously much younger than me, but someone had told him there was a drummer living up at Astwood Bank that he should have a chat with. So the front door bell rang and there's this lad standing on the doorstep saying, 'Are you Garry Allcock? Do you play drums? Do you work at Austin? My name's John Bonham, I'm a drummer and I'm potty about cars.'" He just turned up at the house and asked to come in.

"I never gave him lessons as such – I didn't teach him at all – but we'd sit in the front room with sticks and a practice pad and I'd show him a few things. It was just a case of: do you know this one? I remember him playing on one of my snare drums and me saying, 'For

Chrissakes, John, take it steady!' I thought he was going to knock it through the floorboards. He certainly hit hard."

Allcock was a fan of Johnny Dankworth's drummer, the late Kenny Clare. "One of the points that Kenny was into was a powerful double stroke. It was something I learnt from Kenny that stood me in good stead during my playing career. It's difficult to describe, but he always said that you should treat a double beat as a single stroke, in terms of one hand or arm movement. Even a four-stroke ruff [a four-beat drum sequence] was only two hand movements. He used to say, 'It's all in the mind, Garry.' So I can remember going all through this with John, and he really picked up on that idea and capitalised on it to make himself a very powerful player. But that wasn't down to me. I was only passing on the information from Kenny Clare.

"To be honest, I never thought John was very good, although he was a quick learner. Being brought up on Count Basie and Stan Kenton, I was into big-band drumming. For me all the beat group stuff was comparatively easy."

Garry realised that young John wasn't really interested in the jazz-oriented syncopated style of playing, but they kept in touch all the same. "He came up to the house a few times and we set up some kits in the front room, although it was a very small house and my wife wasn't too keen. It was like, 'Do we really need a bass drum in the kitchen?' Half the time we were talking about cars. I could see why he sought me out, because I was a drummer doing a car design apprenticeship.

"We became good friends, and I remember when he first began recording with Robert Plant in The Band Of Joy, he came to my house and showed me a cheque for £600. He went out and bought a secondhand Jaguar."

LEARNING NEW TRICKS

When John left school, he remained dedicated to the idea of being a professional musician. But in order to earn a living and learn a trade, he joined his father's business as an apprentice carpenter. He would get up at 7 every morning and go to work, and then play in local bands until the early hours. He continued working by day for some years to supplement his income. Bricklaying and hod-carrying on building sites made him physically fit and developed the stamina and strength he needed to become the world's heaviest drummer. He always told friends that if the drumming business got bad, he could still go back to building work.

"I went to work for my father in the building trade, but drumming was the only thing I was any good at, and I stuck at it," said Bonham. "So gradually it was more music and less building, but I always worked hard all the time. When I was 16 I went full-time into music for a while, and we'd have an attempt to make a success of a professional group. Then you'd have to go back to work to make some money to live. You'd go on the road and then there'd be no more gigs and no more money and you were back to where you started. The groups just played other people's stuff, like the latest hit by The Hollies. You had to do that to survive and play, locally. We didn't do any original writing."

After seeking out Garry Allcock, John bumped into drummer Bill Harvey at the local youth club in 1963. Harvey was 23 then, and known as the hottest drummer in Redditch. He recalls: "John was a bit younger than me. I was over 20 and not supposed to be at the youth club anymore, but I went because it was a place to play. They used to have a different band on every Wednesday night, and quite often Roy Wood and Bev Bevan [later of The Move] would play there. It was one of their early bands. They were always laughing and joking on stage.

"I was also managing a band in Redditch that practised in a club called The Cellar, in Queen Street. John appeared there one night. He was a tiny lad, although he blossomed out later. I guess we were sort of wary of each other, but we struck up a relationship. I had been playing for some years, and John was very pushy, even then. But we did hang out together and later we both worked in shops in Redditch. When John was 16 he worked in a clothes shop; Wednesday afternoon used to be half-day closing and so I used to go up to John's house. His dad had a caravan parked in the garden and he kept his drums in there – a Ludwig green sparkle kit. 'We used to practise and his dad used to go mad. He'd say: 'Oh, it's you two at it again. Clear off – get out!'"

Bill Harvey's band at the time was called the Blue Star Trio. John sat in for him one night at the youth club after Bill had a row with the other two members. "They were a bit lazy about helping to load the equipment and I said, 'Sod it, if that's your attitude'... and that's how John sat in for me. I had the van and I had to load and unload the gear every night. I just got fed up and blew my top.

"When I went along to the club I was sick in my stomach to see John playing my gig. But he said, 'Come on, let's do a solo together – I'm only sitting in for you.' So we both got up on the same kit. I played the two tom toms and John played the snare drum. Afterwards John said, 'How the 'ell did you know what I was going to do?'" Bill pointed out to him that

> **"To be honest, I never thought John was very good, although he was a quick learner"**

every night John tended to play the same tricks. Instead of keeping them up his sleeve and just playing a few, he played the lot. John looked amazed. "Oh, I see..."

John then suggested that they make a regular feature of their double act. Bill thought it was a great idea. "So we used to rehearse our solo every Wednesday afternoon in the caravan. At the gig he would pull me up out of the audience, or the other way around, and we'd do this great drum routine together. Everybody used to say, 'How did they do that?' They didn't realise we had rehearsed it for hours. And it seemed like we were rivals, playing against each other.

"Even though John was a far better rock drummer than me, I had been brought up as a big-band fan and could play some things he couldn't do. People would come up to me and say, 'I saw John Bonham play last night. He was better that you.' Or it was vice versa, because we both had our fans – and they never realised we were the best of mates."

Despite their combative roles as duelling drummers, John and Bill would hit the road and party. Bonham would borrow his dad's Ford Zephyr convertible and take Bill out for a drink at night – in the days before the breathalyser and strict drink-driving laws. Even so, John lost his licence. "We thought we were kings of the road," says Bill. "This was before he was married, although I think he was seeing a girl.

> ## "I saw John Bonham last night. He was better than you"

"He used to leave his drum stool outside the front door of his house – there was a concrete plinth above the door with ivy growing up the side, and he hid the stool behind the ivy so he could climb out the window, down the drainpipe and on to the stool to sneak out at night. And then he'd go back the same way. He told me that in confidence one night and said, 'For God's sake, don't tell my dad.' He was a bit of a Jack the Lad but I got on well with him. Some people didn't and found him a bit overbearing. Me being a drummer as well, I took no notice."

USING YOUR HANDS

Even if John upset some of the locals with his brash behaviour, he always had time for fellow musicians, and loved talking about drums and drumming, so Bill Harvey remained in his good books.

Bill was an avid jazz fan, and was particularly fond of the work of Joe Morello, the swinging drummer with the Dave Brubeck Quartet. Morello was famous for his finger control technique, which enabled him to play high-speed triplets with one stick on the snare drum, and also summon all manner of tonal effects. Apart from his electrifying influence on fellow drummers, Joe was also well-known with the general public for his use of unusual time signatures on a number of Brubeck's hit tunes, including 'Take Five' and 'It's A Raggy Waltz'.

"I went wild about Joe Morello," recalls Bill. "I bought all the records and went to see all his concerts and clinics. Joe did this finger-tapping thing where he wet his thumb and rubbed it on the snare drum to produce a lion's roar. He'd imitate a bow and arrow, and also did this African rhythm by finger-tapping that was absolutely fabulous.

"I spent hours copying him and eventually got somewhere near good. I thought I'd put it into my 15-minute drum solo with the Blue Star Trio. So John came along one night and heard me playing with my fingers. He said, 'Bloody hell, how did you do that? You've gotta show me.'"

> **"Brushes..? Nah. Hit 'em as hard as you can"**

Bill assured his mate it was possible to hit the drum with his hands and fingers without hurting himself. After showing John the knack of Morello-style finger control, John was impatient to try it out. "Right, I've got it. Leave me to it," he said. Two days later Bill saw his mate with Elastoplast bandages all over his fingers. "I said, 'John, what have you done?' He'd cut his hands by hitting the edge of the cymbals. I told him not to hit them so hard. But he used that technique on 'Moby Dick', which was one of the first drum solos he did on record with Led Zeppelin." Bill is adamant that's how John got his finger playing together – via Joe Morello.

"I never showed him how to play paradiddles and drum exercises. He was just naturally gifted. He was also very heavy. I tried to get him to use brushes once and he wasn't really keen. I said, 'You should try and use your brushes for a bit of finesse, John.' He just said, 'Nah. Hit 'em as hard as yer can.'"

Legend has it that Bonham played a hand drum solo on the Duke Ellington standard 'Caravan' with the Blue Star Trio. Bill Harvey is quite miffed at this suggestion. "It was *me* who used to play 'Caravan'. That was my big solo in the Blue Stars. If he *did* play it, then he pinched it off me, the sod... How it happened was I went to see Humphrey Lyttelton's jazz band and they used to play 'Caravan'. Their drummer was brilliant and played a great pattern on the floor tom tom with his hands. I watched him intently and when I got home it was still in my head. So I practised it until I could play this Egyptian rhythm. Then I put down my sticks and used my fingers. John tried it too, but he never got it right. If he did ever play 'Caravan', I feel honoured."

Bill kept an eye on his impetuous mate and tried to suggest that Bonham adopt a more orthodox position at the snare drum. Most drummers of the old school kept their snare drum stands at a relatively high position to make sticking easier. "We used to argue about this. I had always been told to keep the snare drum as high as possible. John said, 'Why? I like it down in me lap.' I tried to explain this meant the drum strokes had further to travel. If the drum was higher it made rim shots easier... 'Oh bullshit,' he'd say." (There's more on Bonham's playing style and technique in Chapter Five.)

Bonham was the first drummer Bill Harvey ever saw using a chain-driven bass drum pedal. Instead of the usual leather or plastic strap, he bought one with a flexible metal chain that enabled Bonham to play triplets – three strikes with one hit – on the bass drum. It produced a rapid-fire tattoo that astounded Harvey.

John – often known by his nickname of 'Bonzo' – also used a wooden beater on the bass-drum pedal to help get an even harder sound. "I used to say to him, 'What do you use use that for, John? You'll wear the sodding skin out.'" Skins were expensive, and Bill advised him to use a pad to protect the bass drum head. (Ironically it was Bill who broke one of John's tom tom skins during a heated solo one night; but instead of replacing the head, John simply turned the drum upside down. John then proceeded to borrow Bill's Premier bass drum pedal, and returned it the next night, bent out of shape.)

After all the help he had given John, Bill somehow expected to have the favour returned. "How did you do that bass drum triplet, John?" he once asked. "Ah," said Bonzo airily, "you've gotta have the technique," and just laughed. He wouldn't give away the secret, not even as a trade-off. Maybe he guessed the future of rock drumming lay in foot power, rather than finger control.

"I wasn't too bothered, because I was more into jazz playing than rock," says Bill. "If I had pressed him he would have told me how he did it. I just think he was very clever with his timing and his footwork. He could play things I'd never even think about. He also had so much drive and energy. He wouldn't sit down and work something out. He'd just go for it, with a kind of inner sixth sense to help him. His feel for rock music was unbelievable.

"He did sit in for me at a wedding once, when I broke my finger. He could do all those waltzes and quicksteps but he really wasn't into playing that style. His father Jack always used to say to me, 'I wish our John would play drums like you do.' He'd see me play jazz at the local Conservative Club after hours and he'd buy me a drink. But when he went to see John play with Led Zeppelin, he changed his mind. He was proud of him."

It was this combination of strength, power and confidence that made the young Bonham seem unbeatable. Even when he was 15 or 16 he'd quite happily take on all-comers, as Bill

Harvey remembers. "I went out with him a couple of nights to see a band and the first thing he'd say to me was, 'That drummer is crap.' When they came off for a break, he'd go straight up to the bandleader and say, 'Your drummer's not much good, is he? Let me have a go and I'll show you.'

"He'd get on the drums and everyone would be amazed. So the poor chap would get the sack and John would take his job. He was pushy and he got in wherever he wanted – but he had a heart of gold."

THE SPIDERS FROM REDDITCH

As well as seeking out fellow drummers, John listened avidly to records and the radio, and among the British bands he liked were Johnny Kidd & The Pirates, The Hollies and the Graham Bond Organisation with Ginger Baker on drums. Ginger was one of his early rock drumming idols but Bonham also listened to American jazz legends Gene Krupa, Buddy Rich, Louis Bellson, Art Blakey and Max Roach.

After jamming with the Blue Star Trio and other local outfits, John joined his first semi-professional group, Terry Webb & The Spiders, when he was 16. The singer wore a gold lamé jacket and the rest of the band wore purple jackets with velvet lapels in teddy boy fashion, complete with greasy hair and bootlace ties. At the same time John made one of his earliest recordings, when he played on a pop tune called 'She's A Mod' by The Senators. The track appears on a rare 1964 compilation album *Brum Beat*. Behind the out-of-tune vocal harmonies, John can be heard playing a lively twist rhythm on what was believed to be a Premier kit (colour unknown).

> "Your drummer's not much good, is he? Let me have a go and I'll show you"

He later explained that his first musical influences were US soul and R&B drummers. "It was just that feel, that sound. I said to myself, 'I'll get that sound.'" It was the start of his quest for the big, open drum tone, which led him to go for large drums, free of the dampers and mufflers that roadies, soundmen and recording engineers liked to inflict on drum kits in their efforts to control the sound.

Many young drummers, whatever their chosen style, tended to be rather nervous about over-playing or showing off, usually fearful of the effects on their fellow musicians, let alone the promoters. Tutors would tell them earnestly, "You must play *for* the band." John had no such problems. Quite early on he began to introduce blistering drum solos, often using his recently-acquired bare-hands technique on the snare drum and toms. "I liked drums to be big and powerful," he once said. "I've never used cymbals much. I crash into a solo and crash out with them. I like the sound of drums – they sound better than cymbals. When I play with my hands you get the absolute true sound – there's no wood involved. It hurts at first but the skin hardens, and now I can hit a drum harder with my hands than with sticks.

"I was always breaking heads when I first started playing. Now I hardly ever break any. I don't hit them so hard, but I play much louder. It's all to do with the swing. You get much better tone than with a short stab.

"I think feeling is a lot more important than technique. It's all very well doing a triple paradiddle, but who's going to know you've done it? If you play technically you sound like everyone else – it's originality that counts. I yell out like a bear when I'm playing to give my playing a boost. I like it to be like a thunderstorm."

In the competitive atmosphere of the mid 1960s, the up-and-coming young grizzly bear wasn't always popular with other musicians. Some frankly disliked him and others were jealous. But if he stepped on a few toes during his early years on the Midlands beat scene, he didn't really care. And most other drummers were ready to forgive him, especially when they saw he was creating his own style. At the same time he was not averse to creating a commotion when he was in a mood for mischief.

Bill Harvey recalls him playing a gig with Birmingham band The Locomotive. "John got absolutely paralytic that night. He used to go and do a solo – to start the evening. Just like Buddy Rich used to do. John would get up there, go wild, and come off as sober as a judge." He seemed to sweat the alcohol out of his system.

John's social drinking during his teenage years seemed like good fun, just a natural part of his life as an itinerant rock musician. But he was perhaps unwittingly laying the foundations for an increasing dependence on alcohol.

There was certainly plenty of peer encouragement to drink vast amounts. Brother Mick recalled one particularly extreme incident: "John could out-drink me – and I could down a pint in under four seconds. This got us into trouble one night when were down our local, the Duke Of Marlborough. We were in the pub after closing time with the guv'nor, a friend of ours called Gordon. John challenged me to a race. So I got my pint and he got his pint, and Gordon decided to have a go as well – with a pint pot of gin & tonic. I managed to beat John, but Gordon was only a second behind us. We were well gone..."

Still, Bill Harvey insists he only saw John's good-natured side, despite his increasing alcohol intake. "He never ever got nasty when he was drunk. He would do anything for you. All he would say was, 'I'm John Bonham. But I'll help you. What do you want?'"

NEW WAY OF LIFE

After a year with Terry Webb, in 1965 Bonham joined another band, A Way Of Life – more of which later. That same year, though, he took the plunge and got married, at the age of 17, to Pat Phillips, a girl he had met while playing a gig in Kidderminster. Pat and her sisters – Sheila, Margaret and Beryl – had formed a friendship with the two Bonham brothers, and often socialised together.

As Mick Bonham commented later: "It was great for me, because I was only 15 and I was going out with them all. Pat's sisters went everywhere together, and it was like a party every night. But it was just good fun, going out dancing."

For John and Pat it developed into something much more significant – and long-lasting, as Mick elaborated. "He met Pat when he was 16 and his love for her didn't diminish at all, through all their years together. Pat went with him everywhere."

The couple decided to get married when Pat became pregnant (with Jason). But none of John's mates were aware of his plans to wed. The first that drummer friend Mac Poole heard about it was when John turned up at the Bulls Head pub wearing a suit. Mac: "Everyone else was dressed in tie-dyed tee-shirts and jeans. 'Why are you wearing a suit, John?' 'Oh I'm practising for tomorrow. I'm getting married.' He was only 17 years old.

> "If you play technically you sound like everyone else – it's originality that counts"

"So he lined up all these drinks and got absolutely out of his brain. He jumped on to my kit and pepper-potted the drums. He dug all the sticks into the skins because he didn't know how to bounce them. He absolutely whacked it, which I thought was quite funny, even though it was my kit."

The suit became the source of another Bonham legend. As Garry Allcock recalls he ordered the wedding outfit from a tailor in Redditch called Robinsons (run by the father-in-law of a local pianist). John was measured for the suit, but when he turned up to collect it in time for the wedding on Saturday, he didn't have enough money. The tailor said, "Well it's a bespoke suit made especially for you. You had better take it and pay me as soon as you can after the wedding." The story goes that when John made a lot of money with Led Zeppelin he went back to Robinsons and ordered a dozen suits.

But John's transformation into a wealthy rock superstar was still some way off. When John and Pat first got married they lived for a while in his dad's caravan. Mick Bonham recalled that the mobile home provided much-needed accommodation during a lean period. "Our dad had sold the previous caravan and bought a big touring van, which was parked at the back of mum's shop. There was also a storeroom attached to the shop, which we decorated and turned into a lounge. So Pat and John could sleep in the van and live in the storeroom. It was quite a big caravan and it was fitted out and stocked from the shop."

John and his dad began renovating a pair of houses, not far from the shop, one of which was going to be John and Pat's new home. John had the job of laying new floorboards, and he spent a day hammering away. The next day the plumbers came and turned on the mains supply. Water instantly came pouring through the ceiling.

> **"John and Pattie were always rowing: 'How can we pay the bills?' "**

Mick: "In one run of water pipe John had hammered in 19 nails. He'd put the floor down but he hadn't marked the pipes. He did a disappearing act and went back to playing drums after that."

Mac Poole also remembers John and Pat living in the caravan. "John was penniless. Of course he and Pattie were always rowing: 'How can we pay the bills?' [Later] they moved to a high rise flat in Eve Hill in Dudley, where they were still living when the first Zeppelin album was released."

Even though work was coming in fairly regularly, John was still broke most of the time. Whenever he had any cash he spent it on ale or new drums, while his parents supported him and his young wife with generous loans. But John refused to live on 'hand-outs' and eventually took a day job that was completely different from his usual slog around the building sites. During 1965 he went to work for a clothing company called Osborne's, a high-class tailor in Redditch. It was ideal for natty-dresser John: the man who later became famous for his straggly beards, *Clockwork Orange*-style bowler hat and white dungarees wouldn't be seen with a hair out of place when he was a smart young man about town.

THE FLASHEST MILKMAN

Even when he adopted the rock fashions of the 1970s, Bonzo retained a taste for the traditional, conservative suit. Mick Bonham: "In those days John was tall and very slim. Some people can wear a suit and it hangs perfectly, like Bruce Forsyth. John loved to wear a suit, with a collar and a perfectly knotted tie." Particular outfits carry particular stories. Apart from the wedding suit there was also the saga of the bright orange suede jacket – something of a rarity in the Midlands in 1965. "Where he got it from I don't know," Mick later mused. "By day he'd be working at Osborne's, wearing a suit and tie, and then in the evening he'd go out wearing this orange jacket, which I really liked. He was still working in bands at the same time, but never seemed to have enough money. One day he said to me: 'You know you love that orange suede jacket? I'll sell it to you for a fiver.' So I give him £5, which was my first week's wages, and I put the coat into my wardrobe. I had to go away for a couple of weeks on a trip to London with my mates. When I came back, a girl I knew put on a big party, so we all went up there on our scooters. And there was this bloke at the party wearing a bright orange suede jacket. So I said to him, 'That's funny, I thought I had the only one.' It turned out John had taken the jacket out of my wardrobe and flogged it to this bloke for a fiver as well."

Despite his love of sartorial elegance, John realised the need to appear groovy and hip as a touring musician. He wasn't particularly into teddy boy styles any more, and mod fashions didn't appeal, so he improvised. Mick saw him getting hold of a milkman's white jacket and carrying out some strange experiments.

"The jacket had three patch pockets. He took the stitching out and removed the pockets. He dyed the jacket mauve and then dyed the pockets green, yellow and red. So he was wearing this mauve milkman's jacket with multi-coloured pockets. He'd go out wearing this thing and nobody had seen anything like it. People stared, but he was completely oblivious. He had a lot of front. He came up with all these dress ideas when other kids were still wearing

> "People stared, but he was completely oblivious. He had a lot of front"

Beatle-collar jackets. And Redditch was a small town where not a lot happened. So when you saw an 18-year-old coming down the street wearing a mauve milkman's jacket, or a frock coat made of bright green curtain material, it caused quite a stir."

ON THE CIRCUIT

John had met fellow drummer Mac Poole at the Oldhill Park Plaza, part of what was known as the Ma Regan circuit. This took its name from the formidable lady who owned the business, and whose husband worked as the compere. They ran the Ritz, Kingsheath, Oldhill Plaza, Handsworth Plaza and the Birmingham Cavern. During 1963/64 all the local bands aspired to play at her venues – they were, in Mick Bonham's words, "the backbone of the Birmingham scene".

Mac Poole recalls: "Everyone played on that circuit, and that's where I first met John, when he was still playing with Terry Webb & The Spiders. I met him just before he started to go out with Pat. I knew Pat and Beryl because they used to frequent the Oldhill Plaza – they were there every week and knew all the bands. Really nice girls. I had only just started playing drums myself – I used to play with a band called Cyclones. Later on John and I both played with A Way Of Life – we swapped that job two or three times. They used to throw John out because he was either drunk or loud. I was sacked because I was too busy."

Brothers Chris and Reggie Jones ran A Way Of Life. Chris was the singer and Reggie played guitar. The group had strong family connections with many of the top Birmingham bands: The Move's Ace Kefford was a cousin of the Jones boys, and guitarist Mike Hopkins was formerly with Denny Laine & The Diplomats. The original bass player was Tony Clark, who lined up a deal with the Moody Blues that involved their keyboard player, Mike Pinder, managing the band. But, as Mac recalls, the Joneses were hard to keep up with.

"Before the band was called A Way Of Life it was The Chucks, and they were always going through drummers. You would be in the band for three months and then wouldn't hear anything. You'd ring up and the brothers would say, 'Oh we're going on to a different circuit and we've two new guys in.' It was a bit political."

Even after the name change, the drummers were never quite sure what was going on. Mac: "I'd meet John down the Cedar Club and he'd say, 'I've just joined A Way Of Life' and I'd say, 'Oh, that's funny, I thought I was playing with them.' It was a bit like that. The Jones brothers would change their minds for all kinds of reasons. John would take them out and get them pissed and they'd say, 'Oh, he's a nice bloke. We'll have him back in the band.'"

TOO LOUD

Most young drummers took immense pride in their kits. They scrimped and saved to buy better drums, cymbals and hardware, always hoping that it would improve the sound, and of course impress audiences and fellow musicians.

While British-built kits like Premier were well-made and readily available, young rock drummers began to turn to the more fashionable American kits during the late 1960s. Mac Poole used to play a Ludwig Super Classic kit, the same model John used with A Way Of Life. "His was green sparkle and mine was silver sparkle. He used to treat his kit abysmally. It was because his dad had paid for it. It was the old story – when you're spoiled you don't look after it. I didn't know his dad had paid for the drums at the time and used to get a bit miffed when he chucked this stuff around. I handled my kit with kid gloves, because I was still paying for it every week.

"He was no technician but he always wanted to be one of the loudest drummers in the west. He was determined not to be drowned out by guitarists, which I could understand.

He even lined his bass drum with silver paper to make it louder." (The theory being that the more reflective the interior, the less sound would be absorbed by the drum itself.) The guitarists had their Vox AC-30 amplifiers and they could kick out some noise. The drummers complained that if they had a treble-boosted amplifier stuck next to their ears, it would blow their brains out. At times it seemed almost like open warfare between drummers and guitarists.

Poole remembers the night when John desperately wanted to try out a new lick with some luckless band. It was a half-time triplet on a slow blues. "He threw it in and went all around the kit, but it didn't come off. He hadn't quite mastered this pattern and he kept trying to get it right. The band was completely pissed off by the time they'd finished the set. I said to John, 'You've got a few problems with the band, right?' He said, 'Oh fuck *them*!'

"He was a bull in a china shop, without any shadow of a doubt. He had no subtlety but he was highly innovative. He was determined to create something of his own. I think he only had about three months of lessons ... he wanted to teach himself. He had this triplet thing on the left hand on the snare drum and right foot on the bass drum that he wanted to get off. He'd be playing a soul number and then put in this triplet. Instead of playing the beats with his two hands, he'd do it between the hands and the feet, which was really novel. It sounded disjointed if you did it as a fill, but it was a very John Bonham-ish idea ... His thing about playing was entertaining – he was a natural born exhibitionist."

> "They used to throw John out because he was either drunk or loud"

Poole points out proudly that Birmingham in the mid 1960s abounded with great drummers, but they couldn't "get out". "You had to be from Liverpool or London. You've no idea how many 'sharp shooters' there were in Brum, like Cozy Powell and Carl Palmer – and don't underestimate the guys who didn't make it ... And then, when it did happen, Brum became the biggest exporter of rock music for the last 30 years."

Another regular member of A Way of Life was bass player Dave Pegg, who went on to fame with Fairport Convention and Jethro Tull. Dave insists the band was actually called *The* Way Of Life, but in any case he certainly remembers playing several gigs with John, performing a mixture of R&B tunes and cover versions. "Way Of Life didn't do many original songs. We were very influenced by Cream, and we also did Hendrix tunes like 'The Wind Cries Mary' and 'Stone Free', Creedence Clearwater stuff, the same as everybody else. We did a great version of [The Byrds'] 'So You Want To Be A Rock'n'Roll Star', and a few

Tim Rose songs. And Tamla, but done in a heavy rock-trio way – not unlike Vanilla Fudge." Unfortunately they began to lose gigs because their drummer was deemed too loud.

Dave: "If you were in a band with Bonham you knew you'd never get booked back again. We only did about 20 gigs around Birmingham. Often we only did the first half of the evening because it was so loud the promoters would say, 'If you can't turn it down, you can't do the second half.' That happened at 50 per cent of the gigs, mainly because of John. This was in the days when we had a 100-watt PA system [for vocals] and nothing [else] miked up, and a 50-watt guitar amp.

"I remember going round to collect our money with Bonzo from Carlton Johns Entertainment, who ran Mothers Club in Birmingham. We had to go round to their office in my car, because he had already lost his driving licence – I had a red Renault Dauphine, which I'd bought for £10. We used to get paid £15 a night but we only got half our dosh because we'd only done half a show."

The band also played at the Top Spot, a club in Ross On Wye, which had an infamous 'traffic light' system next to the stage. It was set on green and then changed to amber, as the band got louder. If it went to red, the electricity automatically cut out.

Dave: "It was a kind of decibel meter. John hit the bass drum and it immediately went to red. He cut the power off. We didn't get through that night very well."

SEEING IS BELIEVING

One of Bonham's best-known exploits during this period involved some homemade loudspeaker cabinets. Dave Pegg recalls that he and Chris the guitarist had one 4 x 12 Marshall cabinet each with a 50-watt amp. But they used to see Cream and Hendrix performing with impressive rows of speakers on stage. Their drummer told Chris and Dave: "You've got to get more amplifiers. You need at least four cabinets."

"We said great, but how do we get 'em? We didn't have any money. John said, 'Oh, I'll make 'em. Just bring your cabinet over to my caravan.' He was living in the caravan outside his parent's newsagents in Redditch at the time." This momentarily reminds Dave of one of John's other many talents: "John was always very good at getting tobacco ... he'd often turn up at a gig with 200 Benson & Hedges cigarettes. With Bonzo in the band you were never short of baccy.

"Anyway, I took the cabinet over and he took it apart. The next time I went over he had built another six of these 4 x 12 cabinets, out of incredibly high quality wood – I think it was marine ply. John put the cost of all the timber on his dad's account, which was useful. He built them in about a week, and they were all lined up in the back garden. They were fantastic. He had a mate who was an upholsterer and he covered the cabinets in real orange leather and we had lime green speaker cloths. It made you sick to look at them. It was quite a psychedelic experience. Of course, we had no speakers to put in them...

"The launching of the cabinets was at The Cedar Club in Birmingham. Everybody used to hang out there, like The Move. We did this gig and the speakers looked incredible." There were four of them, with their lime green speaker cloths, either side of the drum kit. But inside each 4 x 12 cabinet was only one 12-inch speaker.

"We played really well and stormed the gig," recalls Dave. "It was like our hottest night, and we'd made it in Birmingham after this performance. I was at the bar afterwards and somebody from some other Brum band said, 'That sounded absolutely fantastic – but you'd expect to sound good with all that gear.'"

NO FUTURE IN IT

Way Of Life never recorded for a record company, but they did some demos with Bonzo at the Zella Studios on Bristol Road in Birmingham – though not entirely successfully, as Dave Pegg remembers: "I was with Bonzo when he was banned from Zella Studios. It was run by Johnny Haynes, and everyone in the Midlands would make their first demo there. He'd just got two Revoxes [two-track reel-to-reel recorders] and you could do one or two overdubs. But Johnny couldn't record Bonzo – the kit was so loud. It was in the days before you had stuff to cut down signals, and as a result it overloaded the tape recorder. Johnny said, 'Sorry, you're unrecordable.' Bonzo dined out on that story many times."

> **"As soon as he got a better offer, he was gone"**

John would always look back and laugh about his early infamy: "I got blacklisted in Birmingham," he'd tell everyone. "They used to say, 'You're too loud! There's no future in it.' Nowadays you can't play loud *enough*." Years later Bonham sent Haynes a Led Zeppelin gold disc, and a note which said, "Thanks for your advice."

Quite apart from his reputation for volume, Bonzo was also regarded as unreliable, in the sense that he'd quit a band without compunction if he thought it wasn't going anywhere. As brother Mick recalled: "John was known for going from band to band. As soon as he got a better offer, he was gone. You could turn up expecting to see him at a gig and he wouldn't be there. He'd be off playing somewhere else with another band. But a lot of the time he'd play for nothing, or just a few quid. He was always hoping the band would build up a following and be asked back.

"There were hundreds of bands: live bands on every night of the week. You could drive to all these venues on the Ma Regan circuit, and if one of the groups didn't turn up – you were on. All the musicians got to know each other – that's how John and Robert Plant met."

One of the bands John played with was the aforementioned Locomotive, which featured Chris Wood on sax and flute, and trumpet player Jim Simpson, who later became the band's manager. Jim, who discovered and managed Black Sabbath, today runs Big Bear Records and organises the annual Birmingham Jazz Festival. Locomotive had a Top 30 hit in 1968 called 'Rudy's In Love' (on Parlophone). Bonham was not featured on their singles, as he'd left the band by the time they were signed, but Simpson thinks he played on demos of 'Hallelujah I Love Her So' and 'Evening'.

> **"Bonham was loud and raucous but he swung, and he had lift"**

Says Jim: "He was in the band around 1966/67. He was always a hooligan. He used to stand on his drums and take his shirt off, and sometimes more of his clothes. He was a really nice chap, but a real liability. Whenever I used to remonstrate with him and threaten to give him the push he would nick things from his mother's shop, like packets of cigarettes, and give them to the band. So we'd forget about sacking him for a while. He was the nicest, most charming chap. When you told him off he looked so worried and so serious, you wanted to put your arm around his shoulder.

"When he finally left we replaced him with Carl Palmer – he only lasted two weeks. Carl had the potential to be a great drummer but he didn't swing like John. Bonham was loud and raucous but he swung, and he had lift."

SNAKES & LADDERS

Despite the huge number of enthusiastic musicians playing around Birmingham, as far as the big record companies in London were concerned there was only one provincial city they were interested in. Everyone wanted to sign a band from Liverpool. It wasn't until later that the Midlands scene became better appreciated, following the success of The Move, the Spencer Davis Group and the Moody Blues.

Mick: "It was a long haul for John, after he started out with The Avengers and The Blue Star Trio. Most of the time he played for nothing, just to get a chance to play. You were thought to have moved up the ladder if you could join a band called Pat Wayne & The Beachcombers." (That group's recording of 'Roll Over Beethoven' in 1963 coincidentally featured a young Jimmy Page on guitar.)

The kind of hard slog involved in trying to find and keep work was illustrated by a day in the life of Dave Pegg and John Bonham in the mid 1960s, when they were booked for a couple of gigs with visiting American singer Tim Rose. (They later joined him as his regular backing group.) Tim Rose had recorded such songs as 'Morning Dew' and had performed a version of 'Hey Joe' before Jimi Hendrix made his debut with this traditional song and enjoyed a big chart hit – and this seemed rather a sore point with Rose, as Dave Pegg soon discovered.

"We backed him on the first gigs he did in Britain. We played with him at two air force bases in Oxfordshire, including the American base at Upper Heyford. I lived in Birmingham and John lived in Redditch. He had got his licence back and so we rented a van to drive to the gigs. We were due to rehearse with Tim Rose at the Ken Colyer Club in London at 10 o'clock in the morning. We drove down from Birmingham and ran out of petrol in Oxford Street at 8.45am in the rush hour.

"We were always running out of petrol. John went off to buy some and we eventually got to the club and rehearsed with Tim Rose until 3 o'clock. I remember he chastised me, because when we did 'Hey Joe' I played the walking bassline a la Jimi Hendrix, which he didn't like at all. He thought we were poor musicians from Birmingham who would never get anywhere – and he was absolutely right in that respect!

"Then John and I loaded all the gear into the van and drove to an RAF camp in Oxfordshire and played from 8pm to 10pm. Then we packed all the gear away and drove to the Officers' Club at Upper Heyford where we played from midnight until 2am. Then we drove the van back to Birmingham. So that was an interesting day out.

> **"Everyone wanted to sign a band from Liverpool"**

"I think we got a tenner each off Tim Rose for that. But he didn't complain about the volume. I think he enjoyed it a lot and they liked it at the American airforce base. It was fantastic for us – it was like being in America. They would only accept dollars and you had to change your money at the bar if you wanted to buy a drink. We were really impressed."

Dave can't quite remember exactly when they played these early gigs with Tim Rose, but during one of his frequent abrupt moves, John took time out from A Way Of Life to join The Crawling King Snakes in late 1965. It was a fortuitous decision. In the ranks of this dedicated blues band he met a young singer from Kidderminster with a powerful voice, an imposing physique and a cheeky smile. He also happened to be ambitious, an expert on blues music, and a charismatic performer. He was called Robert Plant, and he would provide the key that unlocked a glorious future for both of these boys from the Black Country.

John Henry Bonham aged seven (1). The Band Of Joy in 1967 with (l-r) Kevyn Gammond, Paul Lockey, Robert Plant, John Bonham and Chris Brown (2).The Yardbirds made their London Marquee debut in 1968, shortly before becoming Led Zeppelin (3,4,5). Early publicity shot of Atlantic's new signing (6). John Paul Jones, Jimmy Page, Robert Plant and Bonzo hit London in 1968 (7). Zeppelin's debut album, 1969 (8,9).

Stick-twirling Bonzo gets to grips with his new Ludwig maple kit in 1969. Note the cowbell and huge flat-slung cymbals (1). Double trouble – the double-bass-drum Ludwig kit sometimes used during the 1969 US tours (2). Portraits of a serious young musician: John caught in contrasting moods (3,4,5). *Led Zeppelin II*, which featured 'Moby Dick', John's famous showcase drum solo (6). Caught in the searchlights: Zeppelin's striking imagery matched the powerful music (7).

□1 □2 □3 □4

□5

In Person – Zep's UK promotional tour for the second album in January 1970 (1). A wild night at Mothers Club, Birmingham, and a homecoming for Robert and Bonzo (2). Still playing the Hornsey Wood Tavern, London, and only charging 7/6d admission in March 1969 (3). 'Levitate with the Led Zeppelin album' for their June 1969 tour (4). John Bonham powers up Zep as they receive a standing ovation at London's Royal Albert Hall, June 29th 1969 (main picture and 5).

IN PERSON
LED ZEPPELIN

MOTHERS
High St Erdington B'ham
Phone: ERD 5514/4792

FRIDAY, MARCH 21st Adm. 7/6
LIVERPOOL SCENE
SATURDAY, MARCH 22nd
Adm. 10/-
LED ZEPPELIN
Plus ex-Jethro Mick Abrahams'
BLODWYN PIG

THE MIDLANDS
OF GOOD SO
★ ★ ★
SUNDAY, MARCH 23rd
CRAZY W
OF
ARTHUR B
with
JOHN P
8 p.m.–Midnight —
SUNDAY, MARCH 30th
COUNTRY
& THE P
Admission

ROYAL ALBERT HALL
London, S.W.7
Roy Guest and Vic Lewis present
"POP PROMS"

Sunday, June 29th, at 5.30 and 8.30 p.m.
LED ZEPPELIN
THE LIVERPOOL SCENE
MICK ABRAHAM'S BLODWYN PIG

Thursday, July 3rd, at 7.30 p.m.
THE DUBLINERS
THE IAN CAMPBELL GROUP
MARTIN CARTHY and DAVE SWARBRICK
THE YOUNG TRADITION
Compere:
DOMINIC BEHAN

Monday, June 30th, at 7.30 p.m.
FLEETWOOD MAC THE PENTANGLE
DUSTER BENNETT

Tuesday, July 1st, at 7.30 p.m.
AMEN CORNER THE EQUALS
MARMALADE
BOB KERR'S WHOOPEE BAND
THE WEB

Friday, July 4, at 5.30 and 8.30 p.m.
MR. CHUCK BERRY
CHICKEN SHACK
THE ALAN BOWN

Wednesday, July 2nd, at 7.30 p.m.
THE INCREDIBLE STRING BAND
THE FAMILY
FAIRPORT CONVENTION
JOHN PEEL

Saturday, July 5th, at 5.30 and 8.30 p.m.
THE WHO
MR. CHUCK BERRY
BODAST

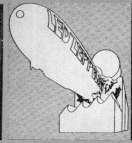

The 'difficult' third album – only difficult for the critics. The band came up with great new songs and a more acoustic sound (1). The 'seed catalogue' cover, which you could rotate to reveal images of a mustachioed Bonzo (2). Bonzo, Robert and John Paul Jones at Gold Star Studios, LA, recording 'Whole Lotta Love', 1969 (3).

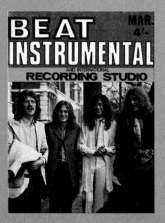

John Paul Jones, Bonham's partner in time (1). Jimmy's crushed velvet loons were high fashion in 1970 (2). Front page news as Zep conquer America and prepare for their sixth US tour, *Melody Maker*, January 1st 1970 (3). John Paul, Bonzo, Plant, and Page in yokel's hat at *Bath Festival*, Shepton Mallet, June 28th 1970 (4). Smart men about town on the cover of *Beat Instrumental*, 1970 (5). A drummer's eye view of Zep in action (6).

Carmine Appice, drummer with Vanilla Fudge and BBA (Beck, Bogert, Appice), encouraged and helped Bonzo when Zep arrived in America (1). Peter Grant and Jimmy Page at a *Melody Maker* awards ceremony (2). Grand opening of Bev Bevan's Heavy Head Record Shop at Sparkhill, Birmingham, 1971: (l-r) Rick Price, Ozzy Osbourne, Raymond Froggatt, Jeff Lynne, Bev Bevan, Tony Iommi and John Bonham (3).The 'Four Symbols' untitled album upset Atlantic but delighted the fans. Bonzo stormed into 'Rock And Roll', climbed the 'Stairway To Heaven and kicked hell out of 'When The Levee Breaks' (4). Dinner is served. Bonzo hammers his gong and tymps at Newcastle City Hall, November 30th 1972 (5).

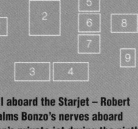

```
        [5]
   [2]  [6]  [8]
[1]
        [7]
             [9]
   [3]  [4]
```

All aboard the Starjet – Robert calms Bonzo's nerves aboard Zep's private jet during the ninth US tour, 1973 (1). Drum crazy – Bonzo hits a peak on 'Moby Dick' at The Great Hall, Alexandra Palace, London, December 22nd 1973. Tickets cost £1 (2). *Houses Of The Holy* yielded 'The Song Remains The Same' and 'The Ocean', among a clutch of new Zep classics (3,4). Jimmy and Bonzo duelling on the ninth US tour, 1973 (5,6,7). Zoso and the three rings symbolise the magical power of Zeppelin (8). James Patrick Page armed with Gibson Les Paul and a rather good drummer (9).

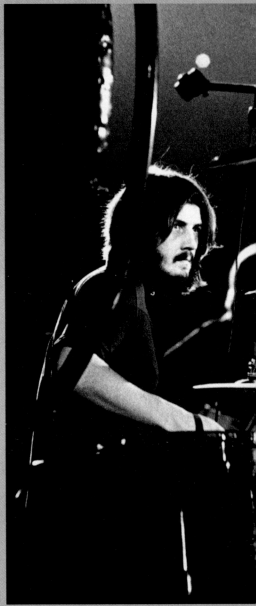

1 2 3 A study in concentration – John Bonham assaults gong, snare drum and tom toms in rapid succession, as he watches the band for cues and grits his teeth in triumph. "Take that, yer buggers" (1,2,3).

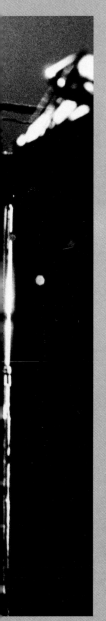

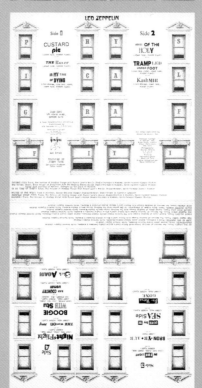

A Clockwork Orange inspired Bonzo's bowler hat and boiler suit outfit, worn at Madison Square Garden, New York in February 1975. He played on a Ludwig Amber Vistalite kit with a 26-inch bass drum (1). The Vistalite kit was auctioned in London in 1997 (2). *Physical Graffiti*, Zep's 1975 double whammy, had Bonzo at his most dynamic on 'Trampled Underfoot' and 'Kashmir' (3,4,5). John Bonham, Alex Higgins, Jack Bonham and David Hadley (l-r) at a memorable snooker tournament, Birmingham 1976 (6).

1			4
2	3		5

"Hey mama!" – Robert Plant, hands on hips, calls Jimmy Page to attention as the band inflames young Americans during the tenth US tour, 1975 (1). Robert Plant flaunts "Granny's old knickers", as he used to call his favourite stage-wear (2). And there were only *four* of 'em… The 'heavy metal behemoth' that so alarmed 'serious' rock critics (3). Bonzo has more fun – drumming with the world's greatest rock band isn't such a bad gig (4). The famous 1975 black & white swirl Ludwig Vistalite kit, once owned but never played by Bonzo, renovated and put up for auction in 2001 (5).

1	2		4	5
3				
				6

Presence (1976) marked a new era for Zeppelin, with a more modern style – evident on the remarkable 'Achilles Last Stand', which featured some of Bonham's finest ensemble drumming (1,2). The strange 'obelisk' that pops up amid everyday scenes on the cover was going to provide the album's title (3). *The Song Remains The Same,* the double soundtrack album from the 1976 movie, with a live version of 'Moby Dick' (4,5). Bonzo thrashing a metallic kit at Madison Square Garden, 1977 (6).

It's a long way from Redditch
youth club... When a man has
been working hard for nearly
three hours, pounding the drums
for Led Zeppelin on stage at
Madison Square Garden, he
deserves a drink. Bonzo enjoys
the pause that refreshes,
standing to attention beside his
kit like a marine who's just
completed a successful mission:
"Audience knocked out – Sir!".
This was the scene in New York
City on June 14th 1977 during the
band's 11th and, as it turned out,
last US tour.

Amazingly, Bonham never actually blew Jimmy Page into the audience, despite years spent bombarding him with a thunder of drums, only inches from the back of his head (1). Page moves to a safe distance as he unleashes the double-neck Gibson, while Bonzo kicks ass (2). More scenes from the 1977 US tour: Bonham drags on a ciggie and Jimmy holds on to his embroidered satin pants as the fans turn cartwheels across the floor (3). Relax, it's the acoustic set – an old tambourine won't let you down (4).

1   2

Led Zeppelin had been away from home for a long time when they came to Knebworth, Hertfordshire, England, to play two historic shows on August 4th and 11th 1979. It was the first time many of their younger British fans had seen them – and it would also be the last. John Paul Jones, Robert Plant, Jimmy Page and John Bonham gather in the long grass for one more group publicity shot (1). It was dark, it was powerful but Knebworth wasn't quite the magical performance the faithful expected (2).

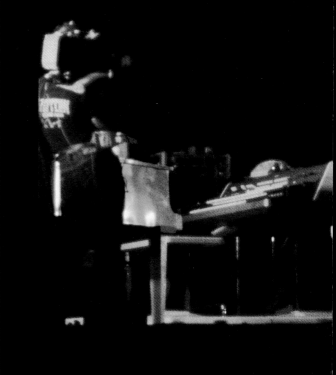

The band on their last European tour, at the Ahoyhallen, Rotterdam, Netherlands on June 21th 1980 (1). Scenes from the covers for *In Through The Out Door* the band's last studio album, released in August 1979. John brought a new kind of driving rhythm to tracks like 'Hot Dog' and the unusual 'Carouselambra' (2,3). *Coda* was released after the group broke up in December 1980. It featured 'Bonzo's Montreaux', included as a special tribute to John (4). "So I'm too loud, eh?" Bonzo has the last laugh. (5).

THE STAIRWAY TO HEAVEN

CHAPTER 2

I was pretty shy. I thought the best thing was not to say much but suss it all out. We had a play and it went quite well.

JOHN BONHAM, ON HIS FIRST REHEARSAL WITH PAGE, PLANT AND JONES

Plant and Bonham got on famously, but there was always a deal of chaff and banter in their relationship – they'd even sometimes come to blows. "Either we got on really well or really badly," Plant recalls. "He was really flash, a little whiz-kid, and so was I ... Because of our outgoing, gregarious natures we terrorised other musicians if we didn't think they were any good."

"It wasn't hostile banter," Plant explains. "It was kind of stuff between kids, growing up among the same musicians. I think the whole thing about Bonzo and I was that we were always trying to prove something ... John came up to me at a gig once and said, 'You're only half as good a singer as I am a drummer,' with his typical understatement."

Having an impish sense of humour, teenage ex-Grammar school boy Plant loved to bait Bonzo in return: he delighted in offering the drummer a banana after a particularly strenuous drum solo – insinuating, no doubt, that his chum had all the physical stamina and subtlety of King Kong.

Robert Anthony Plant was just a few months younger than Bonham, born on August 20th 1948, in West Bromwich, Staffordshire. His father was a civil engineer, and it was hoped that Robert would become a chartered accountant. But he was much more interested in music, and picked up kazoo, harmonica and washboard during the 1950s craze for skiffle music.

Quite early on Plant developed a real appreciation for authentic blues and became an expert on the work of such artists as Memphis Minnie, Skip James and Bukka White. He began listening to Robert Johnson records from the age of 15, and also liked Buddy Guy and Willie Dixon, when his classmates thought Billy Fury and Cliff Richard were the greatest thing. But his life wasn't entirely devoted to the blues. As a kid he was mad about girls and football. Clearly his lifelong tastes were established at an early age.

By the time he played with Bonham in the Crawling King Snakes, Plant had already been in several bands: one of his earliest public appearances was playing harmonica with the Delta Blues Band at the Seven Stars in Stourbridge; and his first singing appearance was with Andy Long & The Original Jurymen, when he 'depped' (deputised) for the lead singer at a gig in Leicester in 1963. He then spent some more time with the Delta Blues Band, followed by a stint with the New Memphis Bluesbreakers. These were pick-up groups with a floating personnel, so he moved rapidly over the next few months, switching from the Brum Beats to the Sounds Of Blue.

Much to his parents' dismay, Robert obviously preferred devoting more energy to playing in bands than studying. He soon abandoned his studies altogether, grew his hair long, and left home at 16. By 1964 he was singing and playing guitar with Black Snake Moan. Next came The Banned (1964/65) and then Plant joined The Crawling King Snakes in late 1965. Pop music was becoming heavier and funkier, as soul records by contemporary stars Otis Redding and Wilson Pickett began to affect the UK scene. It certainly made sense for the Snakes to bring in a hard rocking drummer like John 'Bonzo' Bonham.

Although this was the first time the pair worked together, Robert has said that he'd first met Bonzo when they were both 15 years old. Reminiscing about those days, Plant explained: "We grew up around the same things, and dated the same women. John was very colourful to be around. We were both proud owners of unbelievably huge egos. I was going to be the greatest singer in the area where I lived, and he was definitely going to be the best drummer. The two of us in the same room often made it impossible for anybody else to get in because of our egos and our personalities and our aggressive natures. It was very hard for anybody else to stomach."

ON THE MOVE

After a few hectic months with the Crawling King Snakes, Bonzo left to rejoin Way Of Life in 1966. It would not be long before Plant and Bonham would be reunited, but during that same year John switched to the Nicky James Movement. This was a band that at some stage during its career included Mike Pinder, the Moody Blues keyboard player, and The Move's Roy Wood on guitar. The leader of The Movement was a talented vocalist, whose fame had spread to London – Nicky was originally with Denny Laine & The Diplomats, and according to those who remembered the group, he sounded "exactly like Elvis Presley".

Bonham himself recalled: "Nicky James was an incredible singer ... he could sing any style, though he couldn't write his own material. He had a big following ... We used to have so many clubs we could play around Birmingham in those days; lots of ballrooms too. But we had so much of the equipment on hire purchase, we'd get stopped at night on the way back from a gig and the bailiffs would take back the entire PA."

> **"Drums are meant for hitting, as opposed to being tickled"**

The drummer from whom John took over in the Nicky James Movement was none other than Bev Bevan, later of The Move and The Electric Light Orchestra, who was already known as the heaviest and most powerful drummer in the Midlands when young Bonham was still learning to play. Bev says: "My first recollection of John was him coming to see me when I was with Denny Laine & The Diplomats back in 1963, and Carl Wayne & The Vikings in 1964, just before we started The Move. I was older than him and I can remember him coming along to watch me play. I was the loudest drummer in the area at the time and if John learnt one thing from me it was that drums are meant for hitting, as opposed to being tickled... I think he used to take a few ideas from me, until he overtook me and became the best rock drummer of all time."

Bev, in common with many other top Midlands drummers, soon began to realise that they had a real contender in John Bonham. Although still virtually unknown outside of the Birmingham area, word began to spread on the musicians' grapevine. Bev: "He really built his reputation with Robert in The Band Of Joy and with Tim Rose. By then he was already a tremendous drummer. When I saw him play with Robert he was doing stuff I had never even thought of trying. The great thing was that he was such a simple drummer. A lot of drummers can't wait to fill in a gap with the cleverest things they can play. John would just leave it out. Some of his greatest stuff with Led Zeppelin was when he left a pregnant pause, where he didn't do anything. Then he'd steam back in again. It was all the more effective, really, for doing that. It's self control – and despite his wild image, that's something he had as a drummer."

Bev and Bonzo soon became pals – and curiously enough the future drum star of ELO recalls a familiar-sounding incident with a certain item of clothing. "I remember once buying a bright orange suede jacket off John for ten pounds, because he was absolutely broke. It was brand new, so I'm not quite sure where it came from." Hmm. We know, don't we readers?

JOY ON THE WAY

In spite of the large number of Midlands venues, and his obvious talent, it was becoming increasingly difficult for Bonham to make a living from music, having exhausted almost 30 local clubs. John had also promised Pat he would give up drumming when they got married. But he was determined not to loaf about the house. He was far too restless and energetic. He'd always said he could go back to building work if the drumming didn't pay, so that's what he did. By day he would go out and work on construction sites, often as a hod carrier, taking heavy loads of bricks up steeply-sloping ladders to the 'brickies'.

> "He knew he just had to get back into regular playing"

His bass-playing mate Dave Pegg remembers seeing John at work around this time – rather inappropriately dressed. Dave had just sold John a pair of furry boots he'd obtained during a trip to Scandinavia. A few days later he spotted Bonham on a building site at the Birmingham Bull Ring Market, and was shocked to see those expensive boots being worn while the owner waded through piles of rubble and cement.

Each night the exhausted labourer would come home from work and sit at the drums for a therapeutic bash. He knew in his bones he just had to get back into regular playing, and in 1967 he joined Wolverhampton band Steve Brett & The Mavericks – his next engagement after the stint with Nicky James.

Meanwhile Robert Plant, after his time with the Crawling King Snakes, had joined the Tennessee Teens, a Tamla Motown-influenced group, renamed Listen in 1966. At the age of 18 Robert cut his first single with the group, called 'You'd Better Run'. He then made two more singles, under his own name, issued on CBS in 1967. Midlands beat music expert, broadcaster and journalist Dennis Detheridge says Robert's first single, 'Our Song', was a ballad, which Plant performed in a very different style to his later work. He remembers when he played it on BBC local radio he said, "Could this be the Midland's answer to Tom Jones?" He also recalls doing "a publicity stunt where Robert was signed up to be a member of the Noise Abatement Society... And he went on to form Led Zeppelin!" Dennis laughs.

> **"We were frightening our audiences to death"**

Plant's band Listen often toured with such well-known groups as SteamPacket, which featured Rod Stewart and Long John Baldry. But by now Robert was anxious to develop his talents as a writer and form his own group. He put together the first version of Band Of Joy in January 1967. (At least two more versions were established over the next few years.) He was actually sacked from the first version for daring to tell the drummer he was slowing down. These groups took on board all sorts of influences from Tamla and blues to early reggae, bluebeat and West Coast rock. This delight in adopting broad musical tastes goes some way to explain Robert's constant yearning to experiment later in his career, both with Zeppelin and as a solo artist.

It was at the height of the hippie summer of love in 1967, when the phrase 'psychedelic' was coming into the language, that John Bonham joined the Band Of Joy and was reunited with his best musical mate. The members of Plant's latest band painted their faces and wore caftans, beads and bells. "It went all right for a while, but we were frightening our audiences to death," laughs Robert.

Their appearance certainly alarmed the highly conservative parents of Bonzo's old drumming pal Bill Harvey. Says Bill: "I remember John coming round to my house wearing a bright green caftan, beads and bells, and a moustache. My dad said, 'Who's that poof?' People didn't understand anybody who looked different in those days."

Flower Power had an immediate impact on musicians everywhere. The ever-fashion-conscious John Bonham had decided to put his suits back into the closet and get to grips with the new look. His brother Mick looked askance at his latest experiments. "He got our mum to make him an old fashioned frock-coat in green flowered curtain material. He used to go out in the streets wearing this outfit. He'd get on the 147 bus down to Redditch with his hair all frizzed out like Jimi Hendrix."

Oddly enough, despite the presence of Robert Plant and John Bonham, The Band Of Joy wasn't a huge success on their live gigs, as Bev Bevan recalls. "Audiences found Robert was being a bit too experimental. With Denny Laine and Carl Wayne, our bands were just playing the hits and what people wanted to hear. We'd play a lot of Beatles stuff and the audience really loved that. It was the easy option. But Robert and the Band Of Joy were doing stuff that was much heavier. It was quite bluesy, but they weren't playing Top 40 stuff and they didn't always go down that well with audiences."

MEGABUCKS – £40 A WEEK

Robert Plant persevered with The Band Of Joy, and even bought a van so he could drive them to gigs, although they could only manage about two a week. They began playing tunes by Moby Grape and Love, and travelled as far afield as London to play underground clubs like Middle Earth, where they once shared a bill with Ten Years After and Fairport Convention.

The Band Of Joy was certainly wowing other musicians. One night they were booked to play at The Belfry in Birmingham and opened up for Cozy Powell's band The Youngbloods. When Cozy heard Bonham play for the first time he was blown away – he couldn't believe what he was doing with those right-foot triplets. Cozy was certainly influenced by Bonzo's hell-for-leather approach. "Bonham and I used to get banned from most nightclubs because we couldn't play quietly enough for the punters," Cozy recalled later. "So very quickly both of us got a reputation: 'Not Bonham or Powell – they're too loud!'" (Cozy went on to play with Jeff Beck, Rainbow, The Michael Schenker Group, and Black Sabbath. He died in a car crash in 1998.)

Robert's band was earning a reasonable £60 a gig, but it still wasn't enough to live on. Robert sometimes worked as a labourer, laying asphalt on the roads, and his girlfriend Maureen did her bit to keep them financially afloat with her day job.

"I laid the asphalt on half of West Bromwich high street," recalled Robert. All he got for his pains was six shillings an hour, big biceps and an emergency tax code. "All the navvies [full-time labourers] called me 'the pop singer'. It was really funny."

Despite all his struggles, Robert couldn't keep the Band Of Joy going and it finally split up in May 1968. John Bonham stomped off in search of work, and it was after this he teamed up again with Dave Pegg to back Tim Rose on a full UK tour. Singer-songwriter Rose spent a lot of time touring Britain, and during 1967 Aynsley Dunbar's Retaliation had backed him on a few dates. When John joined Tim's backing group it seemed like a

big step up. "He was on 40 quid a week with Tim Rose, which was like mega-bucks," recalled Mick Bonham. "He was still working as a chippie [carpenter] with me in dad's company, so you can imagine that an extra 40 quid seemed like a hell of a lot of money.

"Although Tim had recorded 'Morning Dew' he still wasn't that big in England, so they worked mainly pubs and clubs. At least the music press covered the gigs, and John got a few mentions, so this was the big time..."

> "Page had a manager, a name, and the promise of a record contract"

When the dates were finished, Dave Pegg planned a band with Kevin Gammon and Robert Plant. They talked about it for two or three days but never got as far as a rehearsal. Pegg says: "Everyone in Birmingham was desperate to get out and join successful bands. Everyone wanted to move to London, and we went our separate ways. John played with Chris Farlowe. I went off to join the Ian Campbell Folk Group, which was in a completely different musical direction, and I started playing double bass and mandolin."

But John Bonham – the man who threw his drums out of the window when he wanted to pack up quickly, and who had spent years jamming with unknown bands – was about to become rich and famous. Pegg felt he deserved it. After all, he'd paid his dues.

PAGE, JONES AND PETER GRANT

During the summer of 1968 momentous events were taking place down south. A slender young blues-rock guitarist with dark curly hair was planning a new band. A mountainous manager who weighed over 18 stones and sported a ferocious moustache was helping him with his exciting venture.

Jimmy Page (born January 9th, 1944, Heston, Middlesex) had been playing lead guitar in The Yardbirds. The guitarist had joined the group in 1966, after a few years as a top-notch session guitarist, and worked for a while alongside Jeff Beck. Then Beck had quit to form his own group with Rod Stewart and Ronnie Wood. Page toured the States with The Yardbirds for a couple of years and formed a working relationship with Peter Grant, the only manager who had ever earned them any money. Grant was an indomitable, larger than life figure. Raised in Battersea, south London, he was a former wrestler, movie actor and security man. Tough, ruthless and charming, he had worked as a tour manager for the rock'n'roll stars of the 1950s, including Chuck Berry, Little Richard and Gene Vincent. He had also travelled to America with The Animals and managed pop groups like The

> ## "He wanted a really heavy bunch that would wipe the floor with the competition"

New Vaudeville Band. He had seen how many artists were ripped off by record companies and promoters and was determined that anyone he handled was fairly treated and got the money they deserved. He would take his percentage – but by ensuring the promoters paid up, both band and manager got well paid.

He was too late to save The Yardbirds from extinction. The R&B pioneers, fronted by singer Keith Relf and originally featuring lead guitarist Eric Clapton, had been going since 1963 and, despite many hit records and endless tours of the US, had never earned any real money until Peter took charge in 1968. By then the remaining original members were exhausted and dispirited. After one last tour they broke up. Page was left wondering what to do next. He didn't really want to return to the session work that had established his reputation. After discussions with Grant during August, it was decided that Jimmy would form his own band and Peter would secure them a record contract.

When The Who got wind of the plan, Keith Moon said they would go down "like a lead balloon". John Entwistle added it would be "more like a lead Zeppelin". When Page was casting about for a name, he chose Entwistle's phrase. Peter Grant changed the spelling to 'Led' to avoid any confusion about the pronunciation.

Page had a manager, a name, and the promise of a record contract. All he needed now were some first-class musicians. He wanted a really heavy bunch that would wipe the floor with the competition and make up for the deficiencies of his former group.

He had already promised a gig to bass player and arranger John Paul Jones, a buddy from his session-work days, who'd also played on the Yardbirds 1967 album *Little Games*. Jones (born John Baldwin, January 3rd, 1946 in Sidcup, Kent) had learnt to play piano as a youngster and later switched to bass. On leaving school he joined ex-Shadows Jet Harris and Tony Meehan in 1963, touring with their band for 18 months. He then worked as a session musician and producer from 1964 to 1968 with artists such as Lulu, the Rolling Stones and Donovan. He became musical director for Mickie Most, who ran the RAK production company with Peter Grant, and who describes Jones as "a genius". Page's other original choices for his new band were the singer Terry Reid and Procol Harum's drummer BJ Wilson. But Reid wanted to be a solo artist and turned down the offer. Not a great career decision. Still, Terry recommended that Grant and Page try out a young, unknown singer from Birmingham he'd seen performing in London. Robert Plant had been gigging with Alexis Korner since the Band Of Joy broke up and was doing other odd gigs. So they travelled up to see Robert singing with a group called Hobbstweedle at a college near Birmingham.

When they arrived, a well-built young man in a University Of Toronto tee-shirt appeared at the side door to let them in. "Crikey, they've got a big roadie," Page confided to Grant. It turned out the "roadie" was Robert Plant, and as soon as he hit the stage they were blown away by his vocal powers. Peter recalled: "Jimmy loved Robert straight away."

Plant was invited to visit Jimmy at his boathouse home at Pangbourne, by the Thames in Berkshire. They played records, checked out each other's musical tastes and decided they could work together. Robert also solved the drummer problem by recommending John Bonham – although it turned out to be quite hard to find him. John was touring with Tim Rose and had some gigs lined up with Chris Farlowe. Joe Cocker was also interested in hiring him. As John didn't have a working telephone at home, Peter Grant bombarded him with telegrams trying to convince him to join the band, which was temporarily renamed The New Yardbirds for contractual reasons. They had gigs in Scandinavia lined up, left over from the old band.

> "We felt we could start again, and change the name"

Robert says: "I knew there was really only one drummer I'd ever seen that was any good and that was John ... [but] he was working with Tim Rose and earning some money, and I had to persuade him it was going to be big."

Mac Poole remembers it slightly differently. He claims he saw Robert at a Joe Cocker gig at the Black Horse in Kidderminster and Plant had expressed some doubt about who would be the drummer for his new band.

As Mac recalls it, "Robert said, 'I've made a record for CBS, but I've just got together with this guy called Jimmy Page, and John Paul Jones, and we're looking for a drummer.' So I said, 'What about John Bonham? He's working with Tim Rose at the moment.'

"Apparently it turned out Robert was actually thinking about recommending another Birmingham drummer, called Phil Brittle, as he wasn't sure if it would work out with

John." At that point Joe Cocker started his set and the conversation broke off, but Mac managed to shout across to Robert, "Do you think you'll ever be as big as Joe Cocker?" And Robert said, "Oh I dunno – he's good isn't he?"

Mac: "When Rob told me his new band was going to be called The New Yardbirds, I said, 'Oh no, that sounds terrible. It's a fate worse than death.' You have to remember, we were all young kids and we had no idea what was to happen in the future. But within three weeks, I saw John and Robert together, and John told me, 'We're doing some recording. This chap Peter Grant has got us in the studio.' And I thought, 'Blimey, that was quick.' Then three weeks later John told me, 'I've just earned three thousand quid.' And I said, '*What?*' He said, 'Yeah, we had a bundle of money given to us.'"

THE BIRTH OF LED ZEPPELIN

Bonzo was pleased when Peter and Jimmy came to see him playing with Tim Rose at the Marquee in London one night, even if the meeting only lasted a few minutes. "A day was arranged for us all to meet at Jimmy's house in Pangbourne," John later explained. "It was quite strange meeting John Paul Jones and Jimmy, me coming from the Midlands and having only played with local groups. That's why I had this thing about the telegrams ... It seemed like a gift from heaven, you know what I mean? I was pretty shy and I thought the best thing was not to say much but suss it all out. We had a play and it went quite well. It all came together quite quickly after that, because we had a few dates to play in Scandinavia as the New Yardbirds. It went so well that the group became very strong, and we felt we could start again, and change the name.'

Indeed the rate of progress was astonishing. Once Plant and Bonham were on the team, the band could get on with rehearsals, gigging and recording, while Peter Grant worked behind the scenes and secured them a contract with Atlantic Records in New York.

Grant negotiated an advance of $200,000, the highest ever paid to a new group – such was the faith of the US record industry in Jimmy Page. But it proved harder to convince the British, as neither The New Yardbirds nor Led Zeppelin meant very much in the autumn of 1968 when the band began playing its first local gigs. Few promoters wanted to book them and Grant had a struggle to get agents or the press out to see them, leaving him feeling frustrated and angry. Still, he had his sights set on America, where he knew audiences were geared up to appreciate the new kind of frantic, heavy rock.

Jimmy Page, Robert Plant, John Paul Jones and John Bonham. It was a unique combination of talented individuals. They sparked off each other and created a rare musical chemistry, from the moment they first jammed together. Bonham and Jones were to go on to form the legendary Zeppelin rhythm section, so it was crucial from the start that they were compatible. It wasn't a foregone conclusion. John Paul was a gentleman rather than a rock'n'roller, who appreciated classical music and was married with two young daughters by the time Zeppelin was underway. But he was easy-going, a seriously good musician, and had a well-developed sense of humour. As a result Jonesy and Bonzo got on very well together.

John Paul remembers the first time Led Zeppelin rehearsed together, on a hot and sunny day in September 1968. "We went to a small room in Lisle Street [central London] for the first rehearsal. We set the amps up and Jimmy said, 'Do you know 'Train Kept A Rollin'' by The Yardbirds?' I said no, and so he said, 'Well it's a 12-bar with a riff on G'. That was the first thing we ever played. It gelled immediately. And Jimmy is still playing it today... It's a great number – I really like it."

It didn't take long for Plant, Page and Jones to feel the driving beat coming from the dark and brooding drummer pounding his Ludwig kit in a corner of the room.

Jones: "When I was doing sessions I played with three different drummers every day. You'd get to know the ones you'd have a nice time with and the ones who were going to be hard bloody work. As soon as I heard John Bonham play I knew this was going to be great – somebody who knows what he's doing and swings like a bastard. We locked together as a team immediately.

"We had a mutual respect when we both realised we knew what we were doing. I listened to his bass drum foot and he listened to what I was doing. It was one of those rhythm-section marriages. Although he was supposed to be a loud drummer, there are different styles of drumming. Ronnie Verrall [drummer with Ted Heath's big-band] was always loud. John was

> **"He was loud from the bottom up ... which is how I like it, being a bass player"**

musically loud. He was a strong drummer, and we were playing rock'n'roll – you don't want somebody tapping about. He was loud from the bottom up, if you know what I mean. Which is how I like it, being a bass player."

John Paul liked to hear Bonham's strong bass drum beat as it gave him something to lock on to. "He only used a small kit, but he used to play large drums. He never played a large kit in terms of the number of drums – he only ever used four drums most of the time, and never had racks of stuff, like people did in the beginning of the 1970s. He could do most of what he wanted on a small amount of equipment. It didn't matter what drums they were: I'd hear him sit down on all sorts of strange drum kits and he'd immediately sound like him. It was just the way he hit them, plus an impeccable sense of timing."

G FORCE

Peter Grant didn't go to the band's first rehearsal in Soho. The first time the manager saw them play was in Scandinavia. He was nervous and depressed, until he heard The New Yardbirds steam into action in Copenhagen, Denmark on September 14th 1968 – and their performance restored his faith. He was also amused by the drummer's attitude. First of all Bonzo was worried about some outstanding gigs with Chris Farlowe, which had to be cancelled. Then he wondered if he was getting enough money to live on. At this early stage Bonzo was only on £50 a week. He came backstage after a show and offered to drive the group's van – for another £30 a week.

> **"Behave yourself, Bonham, or you'll disappear "**

But after initial scepticism and reserve Bonzo warmed to the task in hand and realised that after all his years of struggle and practise, this was the band that would let him play his own style and at full volume – just as long as he kept his cool and didn't get in the way of the lead guitarist. When John first got into his stride and started to play in his usual busy and boisterous fashion, Jimmy Page warned him, "You're going to have to keep it a bit more simple than that." Bonzo seemed to ignore this request. Jimmy was annoyed and had words with his manager. Peter Grant came striding over to Bonham and asked coldly: "Do you like your job in the band?"

"Well, yeah," replied Bonham. "Well do as this man says," said Grant, adding for good measure: "Behave yourself, Bonham, or you'll disappear. Through different doors."

Mac Poole, who stayed in touch with Bonham and heard all the latest news, observed that John and Peter had a very strong relationship all through Zeppelin. "But I think Peter must have fired him about half-a-dozen times. Whenever John did something stupid, Peter would have to pay the bill. He wasn't too enamoured with this behaviour, but he realised it was the way John let off steam."

Given all he heard from John about their manager, Poole began to admire the man they called G. "He was the only manager ever who actually said, 'I manage the band. The band makes the music, and they're the important ones'. I thought he was the greatest manager of all time. Most musicians feel that way. Peter ran the show himself and knew exactly what made it all work, and wouldn't take any crap from anybody. John was only 21 when he joined Led Zeppelin, and he had a great respect for Peter – even though they had their rows and ups and downs."

Grant later spoke, only half-seriously, about one of the 'down' nights – a rare occasion when Bonham's performance failed to live up to his manager's high expectations. "We had a gig at the Boston Tea Party [January 28th 1969]. I recall saying to the promoter, John Law, 'Watch the drummer – you won't believe it.' And John goes and drops the sticks several times. He blew it for me that night!"

MAGIC IN THE STUDIO

Jimmy, Robert, John Paul and Bonzo had a kind of trial run at recording before they did the legendary first band album together, *Led Zeppelin*. They were employed to lay down the backing tracks for a PJ Proby album. They practically blew the American singer away with the power of their performance on the track 'Jim's Blues'. This was the raw sound of Zeppelin waiting in the wings.

John Paul explains how it came about. "[When Led Zeppelin started] I still had some commitments for recording sessions. There was a guy I knew who was producing an album called *Three Week Hero* for PJ Proby, and I was committed to doing all the arrangements for the album. As [the band] were talking about rehearsing at the time, I thought it would be a handy source of income. I had to book a band anyway, so I thought I'd book everyone I knew. We had Robert on tambourine. That was the first thing we ever did on record. Then we began rehearsing out at Page's place [for the Scandinavian tour].

"The first [Led Zeppelin] album was pretty much a recording of the first show, which was why it had so many covers on it. That's all we had ready to play at that time – but the sound and the performance was fantastic. We recorded it in October [1968] with Glyn Johns at Olympic Studios in Barnes. It was old style recording. We just sat there with a few screens to cover the amps

> **"British rock had never sounded this good before"**

up and it was a big 'live' room, so everything leaked into everything else, which was part of the sound. We did it in about 15 hours with another 15 for mixing, so it was 30 hours in all to make *Led Zeppelin*."

The album caused a sensation. There was almost too much to take in as fans, critics and fellow musicians absorbed the power and impact of dynamic performances such as 'Good Times, Bad Times', 'Babe I'm Gonna Leave You', 'You Shook Me', 'Dazed And Confused', 'Your Time Is Gonna Come', Black Mountain Side', Communication Breakdown', 'I Can't

Quit You Baby' and 'How Many More Times'. British rock had never sounded this good before. Cream and The Jimi Hendrix Experience had been exciting, but the combination of Page's electrifying guitar, Plant's screaming vocals and the thunder of Bonham's drums was overpowering. In the midst of it all was John Paul Jones' pounding bass, eerie organ tones and clever arrangements that set Zeppelin's work head and shoulders above most basic guitar, bass and drum bands.

Even today, there is something strangely magical and mysterious about the sound and mix of that debut album.

HE'S SO HEAVY

John Bonham's contribution was immediately apparent. It wasn't just those unexpected and impressive bass drum fills inserted into 'Good Times Bad Times'. His whole concept seemed supremely confident and all-embracing. The entire sound of his drums and the power of the block-busting beat was in marked contrast to the kind of pattering, jittery rhythms that had previously prevailed in pop and rock. He was also a player of great imagination. He used all his previous experience and accumulated drum wisdom to great effect on 'Dazed And Confused' – his battering snare drum breaks made the piece transmute into a kind of psychedelic rock symphony.

He would go on to develop this mixture of improvisation and groove-laying a stage further on 'Whole Lotta Love', the first track on the next album, *Led Zeppelin II* (1969). The free-form cymbal work, stomping hi-hat and cliff-hanging snare drum breaks were exhilarating and inspirational. Indeed John's playing on these early albums encouraged many young fans to take up drums. But his bombastic approach intimidated some established players. Mark Ashton, the enthusiastic drummer with Rare Bird (who had a hit with 'Sympathy' in 1970), watched Bonham with Zeppelin one night at the Marquee. Mark grinned and shook his head in mock despair, saying: "He's so damned heavy!" In fact Ashton later gave up drumming and became a singer instead.

With Page's help as producer, Bonham's drums achieved an echoing 'presence', but they were used relatively sparingly, held in reserve for the right moments. The drummer would set up a guitar break or give Robert the space to sing his heart out. He also engaged in subtle interplay with Jonesy, answering bass notes with shadowing phrases on the tom toms. It was this balance between all four musicians that gave Zeppelin its creative edge and made their performances so challenging and exciting, whether on-stage or in the studio. The band weren't even trying to be 'clever' in a progressive rock sense. Whatever they were doing, with blues, rock and acoustic folk music, they were doing it right.

The first album was released in March 1969, hit the charts and went gold within weeks, setting a pattern for the future. It was the start of the Led Zeppelin phenomenon that would see them dominate the album charts, and the stadium rock scene they helped establish, for the next ten years. They barely had time to gasp for breath.

Bonham: "We made the first album as soon as we flew back from Scandinavia. We had only been together for a month. But at that time I don't think I had any idea the group would achieve so much. In no time it grew and grew, but it was at least 1969 before there was any reaction in Britain. We went to the States because we had to. Nobody would book the group in England. Our manager would try and get some dates and they'd say, 'Who are Led Zeppelin?' When we came back from America and the first album was out, there was a change of tune. People went on about, 'Why are you playing in America all the time?' Well, we had to because nobody would book us at home. I always like playing in Britain; you can go home after a gig. In America you have to live in hotels and have arguments with rednecks."

> "I don't think I had any idea the group would achieve so much"

The group had in fact managed to get a few initial UK gigs, still billed as The New Yardbirds, around the time they were recording the first Zeppelin album: they played Surrey University on the 15th October, The Marquee in London on the 18th, and Liverpool University on the 19th. Then they finally changed the name to Led Zeppelin and played at the Roundhouse, Chalk Farm, London (November 9th) followed by a string of club, pub and university dates, including a return visit to The Marquee on December 10th. They were earning between £75 and £125 a night. Agents and TV producers were still refusing to come and see them, but the *Melody Maker* gave them glowing reviews and fans began queuing around the block.

ROADYING FOR BONHAM

When the group went on the road they took a very small team of helpers. Although Peter Grant tried to attend the most important gigs, he left it to tour manager Richard Cole to get them to the venues on time and with the right amount of equipment. He also had to collect the gig money and deal with any promoter silly enough not to pay up.

But Cole wasn't solely concerned with the money and equipment. He loved the music too, and being a wannabe drummer, he became a huge fan of John Bonham. He says: "I'd always been interested in drummers. Obviously Keith Moon was a great drummer and he had a style of his own. Another was Dino Danelli who played with the Young Rascals and was taught by Louis Bellson. The other great player was Carmine Appice." Appice was the drummer with Vanilla Fudge, psychedelic rockers from New York, who were best known for their ultra-heavy, slowed-down cover versions of well-known pop tunes, such as 'You Keep Me Hanging On', 'Ticket To Ride' and 'Eleanor Rigby'. Cole had previously been their road manager, so when Led Zeppelin first went to America, there was an immediate connection – more of which later.

While Richard looked after Jimmy and Robert, he employed Kenny Pickett, former singer with 1960s band Creation, to act as roadie, and he brought along a young drummer friend, Glen Colson, to help out. It was Colson's job to set up John Bonham's gear. He relished this unique opportunity to see early Zeppelin in action at close quarters.

Glen remembers: "Kenny had auditioned for the job as singer with the band, but they already had Robert Plant lined up, and he was much more sexy. But they asked Kenny to work for them and gave him a job as tour manager. He had never really done that job before, but he said he could do it. He'd been a plumber, and he was also a tough guy.

"I did about six or seven gigs with them. I wasn't on the payroll, Kenny just gave me 20 quid for helping out, and because I was a drummer I knew how to set up Bonzo's kit. So I became his drum roadie. I refused to carry anything heavy, though, because I was just a kid and wasn't strong enough. Basically Kenny and I had to do everything. We had a Transit van and between us we had to carry a Hammond organ, a PA, a drum kit and two Marshall stacks. We had to carry this B3 Hammond organ and yet John Paul Jones never used it. He said he might use it for one number, but he never did and it was really frustrating. Once we'd got the gear on stage, I set up the mikes and tested them.

> "They were sort of smouldering, ready to explode onstage"

"We never travelled with them. We'd turn up at the gig with the Transit and set up the gear and they'd arrive later in a car driven by Richard Cole. They were only getting 300 quid a gig, because I can remember picking up the money one night. It was £300 for Liverpool University [October 19th, 1968]."

"Kenny later did two tours of America with them, by himself, in a U-Haul truck. He drove all across America – just one roadie for the whole band. He didn't even have me to help him, as I never went to America with Zeppelin. He had to cope with the PA, the backline and the Hammond. He did that all on his own, night after night. He'd have to break down the gear after a show and drive straight to the next gig. And he did that for three years."

Glen himself only worked on the band's first historic UK dates, including the Marquee (October 18th & December 10th), the Fishmongers Arms, Wood Green, north London (December 20th) and a few other college dates before the group left for America at Christmas. He describes how the general set-up appeared to him at the time. "Grant and Page had it all tied up. As far as I could see Jimmy was the boss and none of the others said a word." In fact, says Glen, they all seemed strangely quiet. "Although Kenny introduced me to them, they never spoke and only smiled. I thought they were real weirdos. They'd sit around the dressing room saying nothing. I guess they were sort of smouldering, ready to explode on stage. The gigs were phenomenal. I'd never seen anything like it. I didn't know what to expect when Kenny said they were the New Yardbirds – I thought it might be some botch-up job without Jeff Beck or Eric Clapton. But they were the most exciting band I'd ever seen. They were really heavy, playing the blues with no frills."

> **"I remember every second of their performance … it terrified me"**

Glen could detect some contemporary influences, though, and confirms Zep listened to underground American bands like Moby Grape, The Doors, Spirit, and The Seeds.

Though in his experience the band were usually low-key on the road at this time, Glen witnessed one incident which, with hindsight, was perhaps indicative of things to come. "I do remember Bonzo smashing up a dressing room, which was the first time I'd ever encountered anything like that. I arrived at some college gig just before they went on and he'd pulled all the Tannoy speakers off the wall. Maybe he'd been annoyed by some loudspeaker messages for the students. They were obviously only doing these gigs just to warm up for America. A lot of the gigs were only a third full, so it wasn't a big deal."

Glen was also fortunate enough, a few months later, to see Zeppelin laying down tracks for their second album. "I remember going to Olympic [studios] in Barnes when Kenny took me down there to see Zeppelin recording. He was delivering some guitar strings, and we popped in just when it was all going off. They were doing 'Whole Lotta Love' – I was there when they actually cut the backing track in the studio. Kenny said, 'Don't talk – they're doing a take.' He and I crouched on the floor, and it was a really long, half-hour version, which they edited down. Bonzo had one huge mike above his drum kit. He played so loud they didn't need any more. I can remember every second of their performance – and it terrified me."

A PIECE OF FUDGE

Despite their fundamental self-belief and determination, when they first arrived in America at the end of 1968, at least half the band had felt like nervous, green kids. Jimmy Page was an old hand at US touring, but everything was new to the two lads from the Midlands, Plant and Bonham.

Zeppelin's first US date was on December 26th, 1968 at the Denver Coliseum. The next five dates were all supporting Vanilla Fudge – who fortunately made them feel very welcome. As well as the connection through tour manager Richard Cole, the bands shared the same label (Atlantic) and even the same attorney (Steve Weiss, who had been The Yardbirds' lawyer), so that helped. But Cole recalls there was also a mutual admiration that grew up between Fudge's Timmy Bogert and John Paul Jones as bass players, and between drummers Appice and Bonham, which then developed into a genuine friendship. As Jones describes it: "Carmine and Bonzo became like brothers."

> "We were just kids, but when John got on those drums he was like a ball of fire"

Vanilla Fudge were used to working with English bands. They were one of the few US rock groups to visit London during the 1960s, and had enjoyed their trip. In 1967 they played at London's Saville Theatre, where they caused a major commotion with their power-rock treatments of standard tunes like 'You Keep Me Hanging On'.

Carmine Appice, a soulful vocalist as well as a powerhouse drummer, has fond memories of those days, playing support gigs with The Who and The Yardbirds – although he admits they arrived rather under-equipped. "We were in England for a few weeks, and we saw Jimi Hendrix play at The Saville. We noticed that everybody had, like, 'walls of sound'. They had all these amps, and all we had was one Marshall speaker and a couple of others. We said, 'Man, we've gotta get some more amps...'" So they borrowed some gear from The Yardbirds.

This was how Carmine and his band had first met Jimmy Page – so when Page formed a new band the following year, Fudge's manager agreed to let them support his act on some US dates. That's when Carmine was introduced to Bonham. He recalls his first impressions: "I heard Bonzo's foot thing, the triplet on 'Good Times Bad Times', and we were blown away. [When] I finally got to meet Bonzo ... I said to him, 'I love that foot thing you did,' and he said, 'What do you mean? I got it from you.' I said, 'I never did that triplet.' He said, 'Yeah you did. It's on 'Ticket To Ride' on the first Vanilla Fudge album.' All I did was 'boom bah, diddle-ee dah'. I did it twice. But he caught on to that and did it his way. I went back and listened to the Fudge record again after that and found that yes, I did a triplet between the hand and foot. But he did it all with his foot. That blew me away. We became good friends on that tour."

In 1968 Carmine was only 22 and Bonham was 21. "We were just kids," says Appice. "But when John got on those drums he was like a ball of fire. I used to do a thing in 'You Keep Me Hanging On' where I'd spin the stick and grab the cymbal with my arm. When he saw me do that, he started mimicking me. In those days we'd all hang around the side of the stage and watch each other play. He'd look at me and go, 'Watch this' – he'd do the spin and grab the cymbal with his arm – so I'd give him the thumbs up. 'Yeah, cool!'"

Bonham had always enjoyed showing off his new tricks to his mates during gigs. Old drummer pal Mac Poole points out: "That triplet he played with Zeppelin was developed with Way Of Life and The Locomotive. I'd go to see him play a gig and he'd shout at me, 'Mac!' and he'd go into one. The band would shout, 'Leave it out, John.' He'd do this complicated bass drum fill right in the middle of a number, trying to impress me."

And Poole confirms that it was Carmine Appice who was the original inspiration for John's right-foot technique. "John and I had heard the first Vanilla Fudge album, and John said, 'That drummer has got an incredible right foot.' We were wondering, 'How does he do that?' John said, 'Well, he's American, they're into something else...' So John worked on his foot. We both went away and tried to practise it up, and it was tough. I tried sticking it into quite slow tunes. Bonham did the same, but in his attempt to get it right he'd fuck up the band. I saw him fuck up so many bands trying to do a particular stunt which, if it came off, would be wonderful, but it never did. Eventually over a period of several gigs he got it off, and you'd see the end result and think, 'Brilliant'.

> **"I did a triplet between hand and foot – he did it all with his foot. That blew me away"**

"Anyway – and this is the point, the *killer* – when John came back after supporting The Fudge [on the first tour of America], I saw him at the Rum Runner [a Birmingham nightclub] and I said, 'How was Carmine?' And he said, 'Fantastic – but you won't believe this... He's got *two* bass drums!' We had been thinking he was playing it with one foot. It fooled us all. Now everyone talks about John Bonham and his bass drum – truth is, it was [because of] a mistake."

In fact, as Appice said himself, what Bonham and his pal were hearing on that original 1967 recording may have been a triplet played with a hand-and-foot combination (the photo on the relevant record sleeve only shows Appice with a single-bass-drum kit). But certainly by the time the drummers met, on Zeppelin's first American tour, Appice was playing a double-bass-drum Ludwig set-up – a kit which he'd acquired in June 1968. And a kit that definitely made an impression on John Bonham, as Carmine recollects.

"When Bonzo saw my drums he just freaked out. 'Oh my God, what a beautiful kit.' So I said, 'Maybe I can help you get an endorsement.' So I called Ludwig and said, 'Listen, there's this group on Atlantic opening up for us called Led Zeppelin. I think they're going to be big.' What an understatement, eh? So I sent them a copy of Zep's first record. A week later I called them up: 'So what's the story?' 'Great, no problem – we'll hook 'em up.'

"John wanted the same set I had, but he had a different-sized rack tom – a little smaller. I had a big maple 12 x 15 tom and a 16 x 18 tom, and 22-inch bass drum on its side. I don't think he went quite that far. But he had two maple 26-inch bass drums. I've actually seen that kit on a documentary about the band, playing some Swedish TV shows."

Tour manager and drum-lover Richard Cole acknowledges the Fudge player's assistance, but makes it clear that Bonham was stylistically his own man, and in reality owed little or nothing to Appice, or anyone else, in terms of technique.

"Carmine was kind enough to call Bill Ludwig [boss of the Ludwig drum company] and help Bonham get an endorsement deal. But I wouldn't say he influenced him. Nobody influenced Bonham. He admired Ginger Baker and listened to Cream's *Wheels Of Fire* album a lot. He listened to lots of other drummers, but I wouldn't say he copied anybody. He was quite unique. Bonham was the only drummer I'd ever seen who played with his hands. And he had the fastest bass drum foot I had ever seen: he did use double bass drums sometimes, but not on the first tour. He didn't use them for very long – they weren't much use to him, because he was so fast with one foot."

Glen Colson remembers being on hand when Bonzo actually received his new, maple-finish double-bass-drum Ludwig kit. "I think it was custom-made for him. The tom toms were on separate stands, as they were too big to fit on the bass drum. The first time I set it up, he did his nut on the kit – and Jimmy Page couldn't figure out what Bonzo was doing. There was so much drumming going on that he couldn't concentrate – he couldn't keep time. So Jimmy ordered me never to set up the double bass drums again. They freaked everyone out." Bassist John Paul Jones bears out the negative reaction the set-up received. "He did bring in double bass drums once while we were recording, at Headley Grange as I recall. We hid one of the bass drums. I said, 'I'm not playing to two of them.'" Manager Grant wasn't best pleased at the idea either: "Double bass drums? A disaster!" (However, Bonzo did use a double-bass-drum kit during the band's second US tour in 1969, and Carmine claims Bonham told him he used the kit on 'Whole Lotta Love'.)

Colson recalls another package arriving for John with the new kit: "A huge box full of sticks was delivered – the thickest I'd ever seen. John would break two or three drumsticks a night, and I'd have to hand him a new stick while standing at the side of the stage."

HOME BOY

When the band returned in triumph to Britain after the first US tour, Glen Colson was working for Tony Stratton Smith (known as 'Strat'), founder of Charisma Records, when Zeppelin played at the Lyceum Ballroom in the Strand, London on October 12th, 1969.

"It was the first gig we ever promoted and Strat paid them two grand, which was a grand more than we were earning. And they wouldn't go on. Richard Cole said, 'They're not going on until I get the money.' And Strat had to go to the front of the house and get the last dime out of the box office and give it to them."

Meanwhile, Peter Grant wanted his drummer to move down to London to stay close to the action, and be available to fly out to America from Heathrow at short notice. But Bonzo steadfastly remained loyal to his Midlands roots and wouldn't move away. Even though John was beginning to earn big money, with the promise of more to come as Zeppelin took off in America, he preferred going back home, rather than hanging out in London night clubs.

> "He took up his old habit of sitting in with local bands, just to have a bit of fun"

As we've heard, he was still living in his flat in Dudley with Pat when the first Zeppelin album was released. He invited friends round to hear it and check out their reactions. Mac Poole remembers, "My brother Clive came with me – he was a good deal younger than me, only six. Jason [Bonham] was three. I remember Clive saying, 'I'm gonna thump him.' I said, 'Don't you bloody dare.' They were just playing, of course. It quite tickled me.

"John played me the new Zeppelin album and I said, 'Where are all your fill-ins?' I thought he was playing dead straight."

As well as keeping old friendships, John even took up his old habit of sitting in with local bands, just to have a bit of fun. Will Wright was a young drummer with a three-piece

Cambridge band called Lucifer when he encountered John Bonham in full flight one night at a gig in Birmingham. Oddly enough his band's road crew comprised Mick Hinton and Phil Carlo, who would later work with Led Zeppelin, becoming Bonzo's drum tech and Jimmy Page's assistant respectively.

"I first came across Bonzo when he was drumming for Tim Rose, before the New Yardbirds," recalls Will, who now runs the White Horse pub in a village near Cambridge. "Then my band did a gig at Mothers Club in Birmingham one night. Both Phil and Mick were with us at the club, so you could say we had Led Zeppelin's road crew. It was a good training ground for them. The headliners were Chicken Shack, but it was the day they had split up, so Stan Webb did what was, in his words, 'an acoustic set' – which was actually him with a 100-watt Marshall stack and everything turned up to ten."

The extrovert lead guitarist did a few numbers on his own and then jammed with the eager members of Lucifer, who had already played their own set.

"Then all of a sudden Bonzo turned up on the side of the stage. This was about the time the first Led Zeppelin album came out in 1969. He got up and played a few numbers and totally destroyed my drum kit. It was absolutely brilliant – I just sat watching him, I didn't mind at all. He smashed the bass drum pedal and cracked one of the crash cymbals and broke the hi-hat and the head on the snare drum. It was just the way he played. But I sat by the side of the stage and watched his bass drum work, which was his forte."

Later Will Wright and the bass player from Lucifer joined a band called Duffy and based themselves in Switzerland. Whenever Led Zeppelin were touring Europe, their former roadie Mick Hinton was able to get them in to see Zep and Will had a chance to renew his acquaintance with Bonzo.

"I saw them two or three times in France, and Bonzo gave me a purple Hayman snare drum. He said, 'Well, I destroyed one of yours once, so have this one on me.'"

JUST BRING A BOTTLE

Most of his former Redditch friends were amazed at Bonzo's success. Some, like Bill Harvey, had lost contact. He had moved house and didn't see John again until a year after he had joined Zeppelin.

Says Bill: "I went to his house one night and he was very worried about money – because he'd never had so much! Even though his dad was a builder and they weren't badly off, John never had much cash to play around with when he was young. Then suddenly he was landed with all this money. He said to me, 'I just don't know what I'm going to do with it all.' He was car mad of course and had just got a Rolls Royce.

"He was on his way up from London and sent me a message saying, 'Come round. I'll be there.' He was a bit late because it was a foggy night. He arrived at the house and said, 'Come on, help me unload.' And he had a crate of champagne in the back of the car.

"Me and my wife and his wife Pat sat in his lounge and started drinking champagne, and we drank so much I fell down the stairs. I was absolutely out of my mind. John was saying, 'Oh come on, have a coffee.'

> **"We had this five-minute drum battle with serving spoons on the table. You can imagine the state of the table ... Phil said, 'I'll auction this one day...' "**

"He was showing me paradiddles and playing them on this polished coffee table, which must have cost him a bomb. He wasn't bothered, and Pat didn't scold him either. She was as good as gold."

It seems that impromptu drum battles were a regular occurrence when Bonzo came to dinner. It may have been a throwback to his childhood spent battering pots and pans. Bev Bevan remembers having a similar evening to the one Bill Harvey enjoyed.

"John and I were invited for dinner with Phil the guitarist out of Denny Laine & The Diplomats. He and his wife had a little terraced house in Tamworth and they'd never met John before. John asked if he should bring anything and I said, 'Oh just bring a bottle of wine or something.'

"In typical Bonham fashion he turned up with Pat his wife and they had a cardboard box each. They must have brought two dozen beers, half-a-dozen bottles of wine, a bottle of brandy and a bottle of Scotch. There was just so much booze. But then we did proceed to drink quite a lot of it, and we ended up round the dinner table, pretty smashed.

"John and I had this five-minute drum battle with serving spoons on the table. You can imagine the state of the table when they took the cloth off next day. It was totally covered in dents and scratches. But our hosts saw the funny side and didn't care. Phil actually said, 'I'll auction this at Sotheby's one day.'"

Fun evenings out in Tamworth and Dudley were destined to be superseded by wild nights of excess in Hollywood and New York. Led Zeppelin were the biggest rock attraction in the world and duty called. In their first full year together they played four tours of America and four tours of the UK. With the sound of 'Dazed And Confused', 'Communication Breakdown' and 'Whole Lotta Love' ringing in his ears, John Bonham had a lot more sticks to break yet in the cause of rock'n'roll.

GOOD TIMES... BAD TIMES

CHAPTER 3

John Bonham was a great musician.
That's the way I really feel about him,
and that's what I miss.

JOHN PAUL JONES

John Bonham's impact should not be underestimated. His work remains a powerful influence on musicians and producers in modern rock and dance music. He had his detractors: many decried what they perceived as merely loud and simplistic drumming. Yet his 'simplicity' concealed a complexity and subtlety that, by today's standards, are positively sophisticated.

Bonham's drums invariably had something important to contribute to the structure, rhythm and mood of a song. Even when the drums 'laid out', his grand return to the fray only heightened the tension and sense of drama. Just like the jazz drummers he'd heard in his youth, Bonham played for the band. He used every conceivable means of adding timbre and nuance: gongs, ride cymbals, hi-hats, even timpani were all brought into play at the vital moment. Considering Bonham's image as a heavy hitter, he could be remarkably sensitive. Just like the man himself.

But touring made heavy demands on his nerves and stamina. As the band's popularity grew and their repertoire expanded, so their set grew longer. Sweat pouring, hair plastered over his eyes, staring balefully, Bonham in action was a formidable spectacle. He would literally roar "like a bear", as he put it, while attacking his kit, bringing life to 'Immigrant Song', 'Black Dog', 'Rock And Roll', 'The Song Remains The Same' and all the other Zeppelin blockbusters.

He was also expected to play a full solo, night after night. Fans and critics had mixed feelings about drum solos. In the right hands, at the right moment such drumnastic displays could be exciting and entertaining. Certainly for all the would-be drummers in the audience the moment when Bonzo cut loose was a highlight of the show. A well-timed solo could complement the music, and Bonham's marathons with Zeppelin became legendary. He'd always wanted to knock hell out of his kit, from his earliest pub-rock days. Now there was no one to argue the toss. He could play all he wanted, for as long as he liked.

As Jimmy, Robert and Jonesy quit the stage, the spotlight fell on Bonham, as he launched into his best-known epic, the mighty 'Moby Dick'.

THE DRUM SOLO

When Zeppelin first arrived in America they were still a support act and their set was no more than average length, around 45 minutes. But as promoters gauged the ecstatic reaction and audiences were still yelling "Zeppelin, Zeppelin!" when the supposed headliners were due on, the British boys were placed at the top of the bill. That's the way it would stay for the next ten years.

Bonham's solo quickly evolved into a much more complex arrangement. During 1968/69 his showcase number was known as 'Pat's Delight' until it was replaced by 'Moby Dick', named in honour of the great white whale in Herman Melville's novel. The title first appeared on *Led Zeppelin II* in October 1969 – though the curious lack of atmosphere on this recorded version is explained by its origins, as Bonham said himself: "I didn't actually sit there and play a drum solo especially for the record. They just pieced it together." It turns out Jimmy Page had simply recorded some highlights of John jamming in the studio, and edited the results into a 'solo'. But Bonzo really needed the encouragement of an audience and the kick of a live gig to get the best results.

Out on the road, his solos often lasted up to 30 minutes and stretched him to the limits of endurance. But he was always aware of the audience's stamina too. "Not everybody likes or understands a drum solo," he admitted to me in the mid 1970s. "So I like to bring in effects and sounds to keep their interest – like 'phasing' on the pedal timpani."

(US rock critic Lisa Robinson once asked Bonzo about the strange electronic noises he produced from his tymps during 'Moby Dick'. "It's all magic," he explained, archly. "Didn't you see me playing with me little black wand…?")

John's solos were planned to include free improvisation, set patterns and a well-structured finale. "I try to play something different every night," he told me, "but the basic plan is the same – from sticks to hands, and then the tymps and the final build-up. It would be really boring to play on the same kit all the time. I usually play for 20 minutes, and the longest I've ever done was just under 30. It's a long time, but when I'm playing it seems to fly by. Sometimes you come up against a blank and you think, 'How am I going to get out of this one?' Or sometimes you go into a fill and you know halfway through it's going to be disastrous. There have been times when I've blundered and I got the dreaded look from the lads. But that's a good sign. It shows you are attempting something you've not tried before."

> **"The longest [solo] I've ever done was just under 30 minutes. It's a long time, but when I'm playing it seems to fly by"**

John insisted he had been doing his hand drum solo for a long time – despite claims by any number of drummers that they had done it first. "I was doing it before I joined Led Zeppelin. I remember playing a solo on 'Caravan' when I was 16. Sometimes you can take a chunk out of your knuckles on the hi-hat or you can catch your hand on the tension rods."

On one occasion the band played a trick on him. Someone took away his sticks while he was playing with his hands, and he couldn't find them to complete the solo. At the same time the band completely disappeared, and there was no sign of them coming to his rescue. He looked around in desperation, reaching the point of total exhaustion where he had nothing left to play. Then he saw the band. They were sitting in the front row of the audience grinning at him – and holding his missing sticks.

His solo would be affected by his mood, the conditions at the gig, and the state of the audience. If they were too noisy he'd shout, "Shut up, you buggers!" But as most Zeppelin audiences were broadly sympathetic to everything they did, it wasn't difficult to summon the enthusiasm.

Once Bonzo got going, pure adrenaline took over. He could have been playing to a pub crowd of 100 people or some vast sports hall packed with 11,000 yelling fans. He was always determined to give his last drop of blood.

One of the finest solos I ever saw Bonzo play was at the historic concert when Led Zeppelin appeared at Carnegie Hall, New York City on October 17th 1969. The show was the first on their fourth US tour, and it was the first rock concert ever held at the venue, normally the home of jazz and classical music. As Bonzo stood on the hallowed stage, while the audience filed in, he announced: "This is it lads. Gene Krupa and Buddy Rich… they've all played here. So I'd better be good tonight."

Indeed, this was the very spot where Krupa had performed 'Sing, Sing, Sing' in January 1938 with the Benny Goodman Orchestra, a thrilling sound recorded for posterity and subsequently released on a best-selling album. It was also where Joe Morello had played with the Dave Brubeck Quartet back in 1963, when John first learned about 'finger control' from his Morello-obsessed mates.

The two-hour show at Carnegie Hall began at 8.30pm, and New Yorkers gave them the kind of heartfelt welcome rarely witnessed before or since. In the brightly lit, gilt-painted hall it seemed more like a private party than a concert.

> "There was a thrill of excitement as the group ran on stage"

The boys and girls leapt out of their seats to shake hands with Robert and Jimmy, and they cheered and whooped with spontaneous enthusiasm. It was a thousand miles away from those London gigs in the 1960s where audiences tended to stand at the back of a hall, gazing glumly into their beer, too lazy to clap their hands.

As I was reviewing the show for *Melody Maker*, I was invited to stand at the side of the stage, among a crew of fellow onlookers including Screaming Lord Sutch, Chris Wood from Traffic and engineer Eddie Kramer.

There was a thrill of excitement as the group ran on stage: Robert dressed in black, Jimmy in white satin, Jonesy in red and Bonzo sporting a leather hat. The battering snare drum intro to 'Communication Breakdown' made everyone blink, and Jimmy's guitar on 'I Can't Quit You Baby' was almost erotic in its intensity.

When it came to John's solo, he made good his promise to be on form. He played for 30 gripping minutes, and flew round the maple Ludwig kit with astounding speed and brute strength. He played with beaters, sticks and his hands, and never faltered for an instant. But what was truly impressive was the moment he launched into a fast, single-stroke roll on his trusty Ludwig snare drum. It was very much in the style of Buddy Rich – a relentless barrage of accents and rolls that threatened to ignite his sticks.

> **Plant stepped forward ... "Ladies and gentlemen ... John Henry Bonham"**

I saw him play many times again, but never with quite such reliance on speed and dexterity. I got the feeling he was inspired by Carnegie Hall and its musical heritage. It certainly instilled a feeling of pride to watch a British musician play so well and receive a standing ovation in the land where jazz and rock'n'roll was born.

As the last thud of his booming bass drum echoed around the hall through a roar of cymbals, Robert Plant stepped forward and paid tribute to his old pal: "Ladies and gentlemen... John Henry Bonham!"

John Paul Jones was one of Bonzo's greatest admirers, but he eventually got used to this nightly routine. "Once we'd seen a few solos we would go off-stage and take a break. But he was always such an interesting drummer. One of the really nice things about the Led Zeppelin BBC sessions [released on CD in 1997] is that normally I would listen to Bonzo either on record or on stage. So hearing him in a live situation where it was actually well recorded was fantastic. I could sit back, not have to work and hear him do all the stuff that made him special."

THE GONG SHOW

Led Zeppelin toured America with Vanilla Fudge again in the summer of 1969 – but this time they weren't just an unknown British support band. Carmine Appice explains: "The band got so big so fast we were on equal billing. We would close one night and they would close another."

Carmine well remembers some of the logistic problems caused by having two such heavy drummers on the same bill. "Bonzo used a double-bass-drum set on that tour, and I always thought it must have seemed pretty funny to the audience: the kits looked much the same, and when the roadies took mine off stage, it looked like they were putting the same one back on again. We had the same cymbal set-up as well, and we also had the six-

and-a-half-inch snare drum, and one tom tom in the middle, and a gong." The gongs, made by Paiste, took quite a beating – as you'd expect – yet Paiste's designers hadn't really thought about the consequences of their beautiful instruments being used in raucous rock bands. The gongs added an element of drama to Zeppelin's shows in a way that the manufacturers certainly hadn't conceived. At the crucial moment, for instance, Bonzo's giant gong would burst into flames.

It was a spectacular sight, captured in Zeppelin's 1976 movie *The Song Remains The Same*. John Paul Jones recalls: "He did that more or less every night. His roadie Mick Hinton had to set it alight. I think he used lighter fuel, and it was quite dangerous, but you heard worse stories about ELP [Emerson, Lake & Palmer], who were always exploding things. John got the gong idea from Carmine when we supported Vanilla Fudge in the early days."

One of the main problems was that the gongs had very flimsy stands, at least at first, as Carmine explains. "Paiste made a new gong stand that was much higher, so it could be seen behind the drums. Before that they had a much lower, weaker, silly kind of stand. When you hit the gong it almost fell over."

> **"Aw, well, you know, ma – they get a little drunk and they get a little crazy"**

In fact, hardware in general wasn't really up to the kind of punishment meted out by drummers like Appice and Bonham – who were consequently largely responsible for the development of sturdier drum equipment.

Carmine recalls: "At the time we had very puny stands, which weren't really built for rock. I remember playing at the Kinetic Playground in Chicago [February 1969], which was a bit like the Fillmore East. Everyone stood around in this ballroom, and the show included Jethro Tull, Led Zeppelin and Vanilla Fudge. Clive Bunker was the drummer with Jethro Tull, and he'd just got his double-bass-drum set-up. So he went on, and then it was Bonzo with Zeppelin, and then me.

"At that point [John] was still playing his little Ludwig drum kit, the one he'd used on the first album. I remember I got some new 1402 Ludwig [cymbal] stands at the soundcheck and John got a couple ... At the end of the night we gave them back to Ludwig – all broken! 'Guys, this ain't gonna work.'

"We used to beat the hell out of them and crack the tops off. We used to break the Ludwig Speed King [bass drum] pedals also. Those rectangular plates that went under the bass drum? I remember Bonzo broke a few of those – so they had to reinforce them."

RESPECT

Given their mutual admiration and similar approach, it might have been expected that Bonzo and Carmine would embark on a full-scale drum battle. That never happened – but it got close. Carmine recollects the kind of impromptu collaborations that would happen when they were together on their tours.

"One night Zep were playing 'How Many More Times'," he says, "and Page and Plant did that 'ah ah ah' vocal and guitar routine, when Bonzo and John Paul would come in and go 'jah dah, digga digga de doo – dum, dum, de dum dum, dum, dum, dum, dum…" you know, that one! We'd all agreed to surprise Plant and Page, and instead of Bonzo and John Paul coming in, it was Timmy Bogert and me … Then when Fudge were on stage, John Paul jumped on a keyboard and Bonzo played floor tom toms behind me on our version of 'Shotgun'. We just had a good old time.

"I loved Bonzo. He was a beautiful man. He was a really respectful guy, and always treated me with courtesy. Even when he had a few drinks, he always treated me with respect. We had some really good times in Hollywood when I moved to LA in '75. We'd go to Zeppelin's gigs when they were absolutely huge and they'd put us on the stage – the Fudge guys would get total access to all areas.

"In fact it was Bonzo who told me and Timmy that Jeff Beck wanted to play with us." After Vanilla Fudge, and as a result of Bonzo's intervention, Carmine Appice and Timmy Bogert joined up with Jeff Beck to form the successful early 1970s rock power trio BBA – Beck, Bogert, Appice.

Carmine remembers the seeds were sown at a remarkable outdoor gig at the Singer Bowl in Queens, New York, in 1969. It was held on the site of the 1964 Worlds Fair and the line-up included The Edwin Hawkins Singers, Ten Years After, the Jeff Beck Group with Rod Stewart and Ronnie Wood, and Vanilla Fudge. (Richard Cole, by the way, recalls that this was the afternoon Bonzo took umbrage at Alvin Lee – as the Ten Years After guitar star was soloing at 100mph, Bonham threw a carton of orange juice over him, which made his fingers sticky and slowed him down. Alvin was not impressed.)

Carmine continues: "It was a crazy bill … an amazing line-up. Jeff Beck went up and played at the end of their show, and the Led Zeppelin boys went up and jammed with the Jeff Beck group. Bonzo got up on Tony Newman's drums and it was just rockin'. Nicky Hopkins was on keyboards, and somehow everybody was on-stage. Somebody said to me, 'Carmine, roll your drums out there, man, and join in.' Just as I stepped on the stage, so the song ended – and Bonzo took off all his clothes, right there on the stage. My mother and father were out in the audience and when they came back stage my mother said,

'What's wrong with that guy?' So I said, 'Aw well, you know, ma – they get a little drunk and they get a little crazy!'

"That was the night Vanilla Fudge decided to call it quits. The whole thing we were doing, the organ-based symphonic stuff that we had started back in 1967, was sort of being outweighed by the new hard rock being played by Jeff Beck and Led Zeppelin..."

NEW SONGS

By the end of 1969, Led Zeppelin were established as the most successful new band of the year. *Led Zeppelin II* was released in October, with advance orders in the US of 400,000. It went to number 1 in the UK and US; and both Zep albums went gold and then platinum.

The new album unleashed 'Whole Lotta Love' on the world, with its famous freak-out routine that Bonham helped create. It was a hit single in its edited form in America and got to number 4 in the *Billboard* charts. (This track was also the band's only UK hit single, although not until its re-issue in 1997, and it's still used as the basis for the theme music to *Top Of The Pops*, the BBC's pop singles chart show – all the more ironic because the band were resolutely an albums-only act in the UK.) Zeppelin had a further five Top 40 hits in the US, including the menacing 'Black Dog' from the so-called *Four Symbols*, their technically untitled 1971 album – just one of many intriguing Zeppelin tunes that sound like basic rock riffs but utilise different time signatures.

Led Zeppelin III (1970) had more acoustic material than usual, but the untitled fourth album provided some real challenges for Bonham, including 'Rock And Roll', 'Four Sticks', 'When The Levee Breaks' and the upbeat sections of 'Stairway To Heaven'. He continued to make a vital contribution to the band's later albums, notably *Houses Of The Holy* (1973), *Physical Graffiti* (1975) and *Presence* (1976). (Geoff Nicholls looks in more detail at some of Bonzo's greatest drumming feats on particular Led Zeppelin tracks in Chapter Six.)

John Paul Jones stresses Bonham's creative role within the band. "He had a lot of input into the riffs we played, more than he was credited for, I'd say. He would change the whole flavour of a piece, and lots of our numbers would start out with a drum pattern. We'd build the riff around the drums. He would play a pattern that would suggest something."

There were times when Zeppelin had to struggle with a particular song that didn't fit the norm. John Paul recalls that 'Black Dog' in particular caused Bonham problems while they were working it out in the studio. "I told him he had to keep playing four-to-the-bar all the way through 'Black Dog'. But there is a 5/8 rhythm over the top. If you go through enough 5/8s it arrives back on the beat. Originally it was more complicated, but we had to change the accents for him to play it properly. And it took him ages to get 'Four Sticks'. "I seemed to be the only one who could actually count things in. Page would play something, 'Da da *da* ... Diddle *da*!' And you'd say, 'That's great. Where's the first beat? You know it, but you've gotta tell us...' He couldn't actually count what he was playing. It would be a great phrase, but you couldn't relate it to a count. If you think of 'one' as being in the wrong place, you are completely screwed.

"I remember 'Four Sticks' was obviously in 5/4 but I couldn't work out where the first beat was, and he couldn't tell us. But somehow we all did it – and foxed each other. We never played it live...

"Lots of things happened on stage to alter the songs. In the fast part to 'Dazed And Confused' John and I would turn the riff round backwards and Pagey would come across and shout, 'What the fucking hell do you think you're doing!' That was good fun."

JONES ON BONZO

When Zeppelin came up with 'Trampled Underfoot' on *Physical Graffiti* (1975) nobody had heard Bonham play so funky. Says Jones: "I think I'd been listening to a lot of Stevie Wonder at the time... We were also big fans of James Brown. John was interested in everything except jazz and reggae. He didn't hate jazz but he hated playing reggae – he thought it was really boring.

"When we did 'D'yer Mak'er' [*Houses Of The Holy*, 1973] he wouldn't play anything but the same shuffle beat all the way through it. He hated it, and so did I. It would have been all right if he had worked at the part – the whole point of reggae is that the drums and bass really have to be very strict about what they play. And he wouldn't, so it sounded dreadful.

"I don't know who got there first with 'Kashmir'. I actually wasn't present at the inception of that one so it could have been Page and Bonzo together. I played a sparse bass riff on 'Achilles Last Stand', which allowed him to work quite quickly. We

> **"We could do anything we wanted, as we were good enough musicians"**

changed tempo on that one – and most rock bands can't do that," Jones laughs. "It's not easy to stop in the middle of a number at exactly the right place. We could do anything with tempos. We could do anything we wanted, as we were good enough musicians. John Bonham was a great musician. That's the way I really feel about him and that's what I miss. Not many understood and loved music as much as he did."

John Paul remembers taking Bonham to see Count Basie's band with Butch Miles on drums at the Montreux Jazz Festival. "He really enjoyed the band and we met Butch at the end of the show. I said, 'Butch Miles, this is John Bonham.' Bonzo went to shake his hand and Butch went, 'John Bonham! Wow man, I grew up listening to all your music. I learned to play drums listening to your records.' So they got on really well."

As Bonham's rhythmic partner, Jonesy was well aware of his unique qualities. "A lot of people have tried to copy John's sound – but it's the way you hit 'em. When we did 'When The Levee Breaks' he was too loud for the room where we were recording. It was a very echo-ey room at Headley Grange. So we stuck him out into a hall and we used two microphones on different landings, which was how we got that amazing sound.

"John was a huge influence," Jones goes on. "He was one of the most musical drummers I've ever worked with, and certainly the grooviest. I always thought Zeppelin were one of the very few bands that really did swing. We always thought rock should have a groove, and John could provide that. The groove was the main thing and that funk thing was really important in everything we did."

John Paul shared a stage with John for years, and recalls how it was set up for maximum communication. "I always used to start the show fairly near the front of the stage and then during the first number I'd move back and end up underneath John's ride cymbal. That was my favourite place, because I could feel that bass drum, rather than rely on the monitors. And of course I could see John from under the cymbal, because he was on a drum riser and I could look up at him. That way we'd play really tightly together.

"And you had to be on the ball in those days, especially in the improvised parts, because the stuff would change all the time. You'd have to watch each other for cues. There was a lot of eye contact. Page always looked as though he was looking at the floor, but we'd watch each other's hand movements all the time. There would often be seemingly amazing unrehearsed stops and starts. We'd all go *bang* – straight into it. The audience would think, 'How did they do that?' It was because we were paying attention. That's how we did it."

STRESS-BUSTING

As 'Zeppelin Fever' mounted during the early 1970s, so came the first signs of trouble. Audiences began to get out-of-hand in the States and there was frequent crowd trouble, even among those queuing for tickets. In July 1971 the band's European tour was also marred by a serious riot in a stadium in Milan when the police used tear gas. Bottles would be thrown and firecrackers landed on stage. Sometimes the fans simply wouldn't listen to the acoustic numbers, and then shows became a test of endurance rather than a pleasure.

Off-stage the band would be cooped up in various hotels, unable to get out. They would be away from home for weeks at a time and the strain began to tell, particularly on John Bonham. He was homesick, and his deep-rooted fear of flying didn't help. John Paul Jones understood the problems that seriously began to wear down Bonham's nerves and contributed to his outbursts.

"He loved playing drums, but he hated being on tour," affirms Jones. "I remember in the early days he wouldn't go to bed until it was light. I used to sit up with him, just talking or listening to the radio. He really hated being away, and he hated flying. So that was another thing that made him drink. We'd send cars to drive him to the airport. He'd been known to order the driver to turn round and take him back to Birmingham. Unbelievable.

"His fear of flying actually got better when we had our own plane. They let him sit at the controls of a Lear jet, and because he loved fast driving he suddenly realised flying was a bit like driving his car. They let him do a few moves, and … I can remember somebody coming out of the loo at the back saying, 'What the hell was that!' as the plane lurched. John came out of the cockpit with a big smile on his face and he said, 'That's the fastest thing I've ever driven.'

> "He really hated being away, and he hated flying … so that made him drink"

"Like a lot of people with a fear of flying, once they feel they are in control then it's not so alien. Peter Grant wasn't a great flyer either but John really hated it. He drank at the airport because he knew he had to get on a plane, and then when he was on the plane he'd create a bit because he was drunk. He was boisterous rather than abusive. He just got loud and we had to calm him down. Sometimes you'd say the wrong thing and he'd take it the wrong way, but we were still pretty close."

It was to alleviate the boredom of being stuck in hotels on long tours that John began to engage in more and more drinking and horseplay. And as the flow of Zeppelin dollars became a torrent, the formerly impoverished drummer from Redditch indulged in a spendthrift lifestyle. Tour manager Richard Cole: "John loved cars. He was like Keith Moon. Although Keith couldn't drive, he still liked to have cars. Bonham bought 26 cars in the band's first successful year in 1969. He'd get bored with them. One day he'd turn up in a Maserati and the next day it would be a Jensen, an E-Type Jaguar or a Rolls Royce. If he'd see Tony Iommi of Black Sabbath with a new car, he'd say, 'I've got to get one of those.' The car dealers in Birmingham loved him."

John once marched into a Birmingham showroom with two suitcases with £10,000 in cash and bought a brand new Maserati. He told the startled dealer that the money had come from three dates he'd just played in America.

At heart he remained the unruly but generous lad from the Black Country who enjoyed practical jokes and liked to go out to the pub with his mates. One of his best pals, who frequently accompanied him on such expeditions, was Bev Bevan.

Says Bev: "I really got to know John well in the early Zeppelin days. I remember one night we went to The Elbow Room in Birmingham, where we knew the owner and were always made welcome. A friend of ours called Nicky was the DJ for the night. He kept playing all this disco stuff while John and I kept requesting the Allman Brothers and Chicago or Blood, Sweat & Tears. He wouldn't play any of our requests, and John said, 'If he plays one more disco record we're having him.' So Nicky put on the Jackson Five, and we grabbed a soda siphon each and absolutely drowned him in soda water.

> **"John said, 'If he plays one more disco record, we're having him' ... Nicky put on the Jackson Five, and we grabbed a soda siphon each and absolutely drowned him in soda water"**

"Unfortunately the water got into the record decks and his equipment and shorted out the whole club – it fused all the power and the place was plunged into darkness. We weren't exactly thrown out but some heavy bouncers escorted us out and told us not to come back for a while."

Despite these escapades Bev was happy to invite John to the grand opening of an enterprise he hoped would prove a wise career move. He opened Heavy Head Records in Sparkhill, Birmingham in an attempt to launch his own progressive music shop. "The shop idea came at the end of The Move and the beginning of ELO. We had a big opening day in 1970 when Tony Iommi and Ozzy came from Black Sabbath, as well as a couple of guys from The Move, and John Bonham.

"Whenever John came to my house for dinner on a Sunday, we'd open up the shop for him and he'd buy loads of records at a discount price. He was very much into his music and loved to listen to other bands and drummers. The shop was a great place for a couple of years, but the guy who was running it had all his mates in and it became more like the bar-room in *Cheers*. It was good fun but commercially a bit of a disaster and the business fell by the wayside."

FARM & FAMILY

Bonham didn't have time to go into the retail trade, although his spending habits seemed to be keeping the Midlands economy alive. Apart from collecting expensive cars, he did use some of his money wisely to buy a farm and build a house near Stourbridge, out towards the Worcestershire countryside. Over the hills and far away from Led Zeppelin, John would lead the life of a country squire.

> "He loved listening to other bands and drummers"

He denied he had any long-held desire to become a farmer. "I was never into farming at all," he told me later. "I wasn't even looking for a farm, just a house with some land. But when I saw this place, something clicked and I bought it."

He went on to breed Hereford cattle, as well as planting trees and renovating farm buildings. The workmen and surveyors he employed were impressed at his skill at spotting whether floors and walls were straight, level and true. John liked to keep in touch with his roots and get down to such pursuits as bricklaying, decorating and gardening. He enjoyed physical work and seeing the fruits of his labours. It seemed much more real and worthwhile than the kind of 'Hollywood Babylon' existence he had to endure on tour.

More than anything he wanted to build a happy home life. After all, it was not so long since he and Pat had been forced to live in a caravan. John said: "I was determined that when we had a house and garden of our own, I would keep them in wonderful shape. I picked up quite a bit about house construction when I was working on the building sites."

When he was home from the road, John had the pleasure of watching his son Jason growing up. When Jason was two years old his dad bought him a miniature Japanese drum kit made to scale with a 14-inch bass drum. A couple of years later John commented: "Jason has got his mother's looks, but in character he's just like me. He's always drumming. Even when we go out in the car he takes his sticks to bash on the seats. He hasn't got much technique but he's got a great sense of time. Before the end of Zeppelin I'm going to have him on stage with us at the Royal Albert Hall."

John's wish was fulfilled – although Jason would have to wait until 1979 when the band played its last British concert and 13-year-old Jason was allowed to sit in. Jason himself recalls: "It was at the soundcheck at Knebworth ... we did 'Trampled Underfoot'. I remember seeing Jonesy's face: 'Where's John?' And then he saw my dad walking out front to have a listen.

"I can't honestly remember John teaching me to play. I remember being shown things – he'd play me something and said I should tell him when I could do it. I'd play for him, then he'd play something really fast and complicated and say, 'All right, then try that, you cocky little bastard.' And I'd say, 'Mum, he's having a go!' But he was so proud of me. He actually got me a little replica of his own kit to play on, and I had to play for all his friends when they came round."

> "In interviews he was never asked questions about his playing ... in fact he was never asked any intelligent questions"

As a youngster Jason was more interested in racing motorbikes than drumming, but in his late teens he played in groups such as Airrace and Virginia Wolf. He also appeared with Jimmy Page and Robert Plant at the 1988 Zeppelin reunion gig at the Atlantic Records birthday party in New York – and played so well he was invited to join Jimmy Page's band with singer John Miles. In 1989, at the age of 22, he formed his own group, just called Bonham, and went on to enjoy a successful touring and recording career, during which he would pay full tribute to the legacy and influence of his father. He clearly had his own style, as you'd expect from the strong-willed son of John Bonham, but he's happy to add: "My dad's sound did come out in me."

Jason also backs up what John Paul Jones was saying earlier about Bonzo's creative contributions to Zeppelin "I know he wanted to get into writing himself. It was my dad's original idea for 'Kashmir' – he went to Jimmy and sang the riff to him ... Jimmy himself told me that. It was the same with 'Out On The Tiles', which was a song my dad used to sing. Jimmy thought, 'Good riff, that – we'll use it.'"

In fact, John's American drum technician, Jeff Ocheltree, remembers Bonzo's frustration at not being recognised for his musical abilities – particularly by journalists, who never seemed interested in him as a drummer. Says Jeff: "There was anger and a bitterness that was starting to form in him. In interviews he was never ever asked questions about his playing, about the time signatures or patterns he used. In fact he was never asked any intelligent questions."

When John was on tour in the States, far from his home and family, these aggravations would mount up, and he would seek solace in drink and the company of like-minded souls, where possible. "I used to spend days and nights with him at the Rainbow Bar & Grill on Sunset Boulevard in LA," says Jeff, "where all the musicians and crews used to go. I remember him saying to me, 'These idiots don't know anything about drums. All they want to know about is the gossip.' In fact John listened to Max Roach, Alphonse Mouzon, Elvin Jones, and a lot of fusion and jazz drummers. That's the thing that gets me about John Bonham – everybody thinks he was into big drums and hitting them real hard. Bonham was into swing and playing with technique. I once heard Jimmy Page play a Django Reinhardt tune at a soundcheck, and John played along."

THE ROVER, AND THE MODEL T FORD

During their heyday, Led Zeppelin criss-crossed America in the band's hired jetliner, playing to enormous crowds wherever they went. One show at the Atlanta Braves Stadium in May 1973 saw them playing to 50,000 people. When the band played three nights at Madison Square Garden in July the show was filmed for their forthcoming movie *The Song Remains The Same* (though fans would have to wait over three years to see it).

The band then flew home, completely exhausted from all the stress of a year's touring. Zeppelin spent the autumn filming the famous 'fantasy sequences' for the movie, which included Bonzo, John Paul, Jimmy, Robert and Peter Grant acting out romanticised scenes. John was filmed at home on his farm – jiving with his wife, dressed as a Teddy Boy, playing snooker, and careering around the countryside on his favourite bikes and cars.

> "I once heard Jimmy play a Django Reinhardt tune at a soundcheck, and John played along"

It also showed him at the Santa Pod drag-racing circuit in America: when the film was finally released, in November 1976, audiences at the London premiere cheered as they watched Bonham driving a nitrogen-fuelled drag-racing car at 240mph over a quarter-mile track. This dramatic episode was intercut with the climax of his live drum solo – a perfect synergy of power and speed.

Zeppelin took a year off from touring in 1974, saving their energies for the recording of their next album – their sixth to date, though the first on their own newly-launched record label, SwanSong. Early in 1975 the band embarked on its tenth US tour, and in March came the release of *Physical Graffiti*, their first double-album, with tracks like 'Houses Of The Holy', 'Trampled Underfoot' and 'Kashmir' all powered up by some of Bonham's most explosive drumming.

In June 1975 I went to visit John at his farmhouse for a chat about his favourite subject – drumming. It turned out to be a momentous day. Driving up to the farm with its long white fencing, the spread reminded me of the Ponderosa ranch in the TV series *Bonanza*. It even had a ranch-style nameboard swinging in the breeze at the head of a long, straight, tree-lined drive.

The day before, John's wife Pat had given birth to their baby daughter Zoe, and naturally there was much cause for some celebration. Pat was still at the hospital and John was alone apart from Jason and his trusty assistant Matthew Stanislowksi. Although John had received yet another six-month driving ban he seemed content, relaxed and satisfied with life.

He was happy to pass the time reminiscing and showing off his cars, the drum kit in the lounge, and his jukebox stuffed with favourite records. He liked to play along to records to practise, including, somewhat surprisingly, 'Matthew And Son' by Cat Stevens. He also loved Supertramp and was very fond of Joni Mitchell and Abba.

John took me on a tour of his rolling 100 acre grounds, where sheep and cattle grazed and the scenery was beautiful, if somewhat spoilt by a new line of electricity pylons, courtesy of the National Grid. Although the cows were real, there was no mistaking this was the home of a rock'n'roller. In the barn, instead of ploughing implements, he kept his classic cars: at the time this included a 1967 Corvette, and an old two-door 1923 Ford Model T – which wasn't quite what it seemed. Closer inspection showed it to be a wide-wheeled hot-rod, with a huge seven-litre Chevrolet engine inside. Bonham had bought it in America for £3,000 and had it flown back home for almost as much again. The big attraction was it could to do 0 to 60mph in 3.2 seconds. Said John proudly: "You get guys coming past in a sports car who think it's an old banger, until I put my foot down..." Bev Bevan was one of the friends who experienced the joys of riding with Bonham behind the wheel of this very 'quick' car.

> "John liked to play along to records to practise ... including 'Matthew & Son' by Cat Stevens"

"It was absolutely frightening," admits Bev. "He said, 'I'll show you how quick it is.' He drove it down to the dual-carriageway, and on a bend in the road he actually parked it in the fast lane. We just sat there waiting for a car to come screaming round the bend straight towards us at 70 miles per hour. He could see it in his rear mirror. And then he just floored the thing. The bonnet went up in the air and the back wheels were spinning and there was smoke everywhere. It went from nought to 100 in about four seconds, or something ridiculous. As the passenger, sitting waiting for this to happen, it was absolutely terrifying, but very typical of John. He just wanted to show me how fast it could go. I was only too glad that he didn't stall it! I didn't say a word, what with the G-force and the sheer terror.

"He always had six cars at a time," says Bevan, "and he changed one of these cars every month. He was a car salesman's dream. He'd come in and buy a Ferrari, a red AC Cobra and an Aston Martin."

Garry Allcock remembers John taking him to Bristol Street Motors in Birmingham and loaning them the Model T Ford hot-rod, which they then displayed proudly in their window. "He also owned an FF Jensen Interceptor four-wheel drive," adds Allcock, still pale-faced at the thought. "He took me for a drive. He put his foot down and nearly frightened me to death."

> **"He drove it to the dual-carriageway, and on a bend in the road he actually parked it in the fast lane ... waiting for a car to come screaming round the bend"**

John's wife Pat also had to endure such trips. One birthday John realised he had forgotten to buy her a present and all the shops were shut, except for the local car dealer. He rushed in and bought her a brand new Aston Martin. He took it home straight from the showroom and took her out for a drive. He went up to speeds of 100mph in a country lane, and she was so alarmed she refused ever to get into the car again.

When John first got some money he went out and bought a much more sedate Rolls Royce. At least, he thought, he couldn't get into any trouble in a Roller. "It was a white one," he related. "I drove it to a wedding in Birmingham. When I came out it looked like a bomb had hit it. All these skinheads had jumped on it. They kicked in the windscreen, and smashed everything else. If it had been any other car they would have left it alone."

A NIGHT AT THE PUB

Inside his farmhouse, John told me the building used to be a three-bedroom dwelling, which he had extended and improved himself. "My father did all the wood panelling and I did a lot of the work with my brother Michael and some sub-contractors."

As we chatted, nine-year-old Jason came home in his cub uniform and began bashing away on his drum kit, set up in front of dad's jukebox. He played along to Gary Glitter records, and glared somewhat suspiciously at the visitor. "You can't teach him anything," John warned me, keeping his distance. "He's got a terrible temper."

In the evening John suggested a trip to the local pub and I drove him to The Chequers in my Ford Granada. We chatted at the bar over pints of real ale, and discussed everything from farming to drumming.

We spoke about his playing with the band, and John admitted that despite his apparent confidence and command of a drum kit he suffered from doubt and worry before every concert. Just the thought of having to power up Led Zeppelin for two to three hours every night on the road sometimes induced a sort of panic attack. It wasn't to do with stagefright while performing, it was the waiting beforehand. Indeed I had seen him being sick before a show, or remain tight-lipped and morose, unable to speak.

> **"I've got worse. I have terribly bad nerves all the time … I worry about playing badly"**

In that interview long ago John confided: "I've got worse. I have terribly bad nerves all the time. Once we start into 'Rock And Roll' I'm fine. I just can't stand sitting around, and I worry about playing badly – and if I do then I'm really pissed off. If I play well, I feel fine.

"Everybody in the band is the same, and each has some little thing they do before we go on, like pacing about or lighting a cigarette. It's worse at festivals. You might have to sit around for a whole day and you daren't drink because you'll get tired and blow the gig. So you sit drinking tea in a caravan with everybody saying, 'Far out, man.'"

As we supped our pints, John also chewed the fat with the locals in the pub, most of whom knew him as a landowner and neighbour rather than a rock'n'roll star. There was much banter as it was suggested he was about to buy the pub. He laughed and vehemently denied the rumours. He liked a drink, he said, but not that much.

Back at the ranch, John cranked up the jukebox and chatted about his favourite bands. Then it was time for me to drive back to London. But John had a special surprise lined up. "Look," he said, "I've got a spare drum kit sitting in the barn. You've gotta have it." I was stunned by his generosity and felt I ought to refuse. As Peter Grant might say, "It's too much." But John was in no mood to argue and bellowed for his trusty assistant, "Matthew!"

While I was still mumbling faintly that he really shouldn't, John and Matthew loaded up my car with a huge great black-and-white Ludwig Vistalite drum kit. It included an enormous 26-inch bass drum that shared the back seat with a 20-inch floor tom tom, and another 16-inch tom tom sat on the front bench seat. The trunk lid was jammed open and tied up with string to accommodate a huge box-on-wheels full of hardware. It was gone midnight as I bid farewell to John and drove home through country roads and motorways to London, unable to see anything out of the rear mirror and expecting to be stopped by police at any instant.

> "After 1975 the band retreated from their more familiar haunts"

When I arrived home at 2am, my wife Marilyne was about to throw the burnt dinner at me until I breathlessly told her all about the amazing gift that John had so kindly given me and was waiting to be unloaded. The next morning I set up the drums in the lounge and pretended to be John Bonham playing 'Moby Dick' at Madison Square Garden. When I eventually played the kit for real, with a semi-pro trad jazz band, they looked highly alarmed at the swirling zebra stripes of this massive kit. The grumpy old traddies insisted on calling it 'the Liquorice All-Sorts' (a popular black-and-white British candy). I used to wonder how John would have dealt with the situation, if he'd had the misfortune to play with such a group. He'd probably have thrown the kit at them.

I never saw John again after that night in the pub. He was caught up in the events that embroiled Led Zeppelin, and after 1975 the band retreated from their more familiar haunts.

In the short term the band were about to become tax exiles and had to live outside Britain. Nobody could have predicted what would subsequently happen to the world's greatest rock band, or indeed to the world's greatest rock drummer. After the early years of success and acclaim there was a seismic shift in both the mood and the music of the times. With the advent of punk rock, attitudes had hardened towards the super-rich supergroups. Even so, Led Zeppelin remained hugely popular, selling out concerts and topping album charts, right to the end.

OUT ON THE TILES

I had to break the news to Jimmy and Robert. It made me feel angry – at the waste of him.

JOHN PAUL JONES

During the band's Indian Summer, Bonham continued to divide his time between Zeppelin duties, working on his farm, and pausing for 'the drink that refreshes'. John began to acquire a reputation for mayhem that rivalled his mate Keith Moon's. In fact, when out for the night, Bonzo was often encouraged to misbehave by members of the group's entourage.

Even when he was behaving himself at home, there were clearly times when the life of a country squire palled, and all the good resolutions came to nought. Bonzo just had to get down to London for 'a quick one', even if it was nearly closing time. Bill Harry, Zeppelin's long-suffering press officer, remembers being in the Revolution club in Mayfair, central London, one night and Bonzo phoned him from Birmingham. "He said, 'I want to come down for a drink.' I said, 'You'll never make it – the club shuts at 2am and you're still in Birmingham.' About ten minutes before closing time he arrived, went to the bar and ordered 50 lagers. The table was just covered in lagers."

> **"They ordered a concoction that included every liqueur from behind the bar"**

Bonham was also at the forefront of a famous 'lost afternoon' in London that also involved Zep's tour manager Richard Cole and Stan Webb, the lead guitarist with Chicken Shack. Bill Harry remembers it only too well. It was the day he decided to quit his job handling Mr Bonham's publicity.

Bill looks back now with mixed emotions. "People like Bonzo and Keith Moon made that era such an exciting time. When I see Britney Spears and Westlife on TV now, I have to turn over... Bonzo was fun, and there was nothing unfriendly about him – and he was a brilliant drummer. But it was a strain, I admit, putting up with his antics.

"They were superstars letting off steam... but when you are not a star and you don't have much money, their pranks can become very expensive – like when you walk into the Speakeasy Club and a plate of spaghetti comes flying through the air and lands all over your suit. There had been a number of incidents like that. It was just mischief and I had to take a certain amount, as did anybody else who was associated with them. But I got really fed up one day at the Coach & Horses pub in Poland Street, Soho."

Bill, as an independent PR, had several clients and he'd set up a number of interviews on that memorable day for artists like Suzy Quatro, and Glen Cornick of Jethro Tull. He had popped into the pub for a drink when John Bonham and Stan Webb suddenly appeared, clearly bent on mischief. Bill's heart sank as they ordered a concoction that included every liqueur from behind the bar, served in large glasses. After a couple of these, according to their PR, "they went berserk."

Bill walked past Bonzo, who called over that *he* wanted to do an interview as well, and that Bill should go and find him a journalist. The PR told him he was sorry, but he was busy looking after Suzy Quatro. This may have been regarded as a snub. "Bonzo leaned over and ripped the pocket off my trousers and all my money and keys went flying all over the floor. He ripped my shirt as well, and I was absolutely furious. I said, 'I'm finished with you. I want nothing whatsoever to do with Led Zeppelin ever again. If I see you in the street, you'd better cross the road.'"

Shortly afterwards Bill Harry did get a phone call from Peter Grant. Zep's manager was very sorry and wanted Bill to remain as the band's PR. He said, "Go out and buy the most expensive pair of trousers you can find and send me the bill." But Bill refused to be placated, saying, "No, I just can't handle them any more. That's it."

SAVE THE TIGER

In fact things got worse on that infamous day, as Webb and Bonham proceeded to run amuck. Having returned to his office around the corner in Oxford Street, Bill thought it was safest to lock Glen Cornick and his nervous interviewer in his room. It was a wise move. They soon heard Webb and Bonham charging up the stairs – they hammered on the door, and eventually knocked it off its hinges, before fleeing the scene of destruction, leaving a trail of toilet rolls down the corridor. They found another potential victim, record executive Doug D'Arcy, cowering inside the adjacent Chrysalis office. Then, says Bill, they grabbed the poor man, "wrapped him from head to toe in sticky tape, carried him wriggling down the stairs, and dumped him in Oxford Street."

By now the rampaging pair had been joined by Led Zeppelin's tour manager Richard Cole. He became inveigled into their next outrage – a scheme to dress up as Arab princes and lord it up at a top West End hotel. Bill Harry explains: "They hired a load of outfits from a theatrical costumiers. Bonzo had been booked into the Mayfair Hotel for the night, so they all went to the hotel and checked in. While they were in the lift going up to their room, they shocked some blue-rinsed American ladies by lifting up their robes. They weren't wearing anything underneath, so I think the women started hitting them with their umbrellas. Once

> **"They wrapped him from head to toe in sticky tape, carried him wriggling downstairs, and dumped him in Oxford Street"**

they got to their room Bonzo ordered steaks for 50 people. All these waiters came up with trollies loaded with steaks and the 'Arabs' started throwing the steaks all over the room."

Richard Cole relates his version of the evening's events. "Bonzo called me when I was at my house down in the country. He said, 'Look, I'm in London for the night. Get a train or drive up.' He was out with Stan Webb, who was also a friend of mine ... So I went up to town, and somehow Stan came up with this bizarre idea that we should dress up as Arabs. I rented a Rolls Royce Phantom 6 and the three of us drove around London in disguise. We were actually barred from the Revolution Club, they wouldn't allow us in there. We also had Phil Carson hanging out with us, who was the head of Atlantic Records in London, and he got us into the Mayfair hotel. It wasn't until Stan Webb put his feet up on the table and they saw his star-spangled high-heel boots that they realised we weren't really Arabs."

Richard refutes Bill Harry's oft-quoted tale about the destruction of a stuffed tiger that was in the Maharajah Suite of the Mayfair hotel. "No, no, no! It was a big terracotta sculpture of a Maharajah and a horse. I don't know how it got broken. Quite possibly somebody was trying to ride on it. Anyway it ended up in pieces on the marble floor.

"The most hysterical thing was we drove past the Albert Hall and saw our secretary walking down the street. So we pulled the doors open, jumped out and threw her into the back of the car. She had no idea it was us, but she didn't resist or screech. She thought it was her lucky night...

"The next day we got a call from Stan Webb. He said, 'Hey, you've got my clothes.' He woke up somewhere and all he had to wear was his rented outfit. He didn't have any money for a cab so he had to get on the tube [underground train] still dressed as an Arab and go back to the Mayfair to pick up his trousers."

> **"It wasn't a nightly occurrence ... it didn't happen in every hotel we went to"**

Bill Harry reckons that when Bonham's flying circus reached the Speakeasy, they began lifting up their robes again, and nobody took any notice. "They'd seen it all before! But after that Bonzo was banned from every hotel in London."

Richard Cole insists that Bonham wasn't always misbehaving, and even on long tours of America there was far less mayhem than might be expected. "The only time John would wreck a hotel room was if he'd had an argument on the phone, or maybe he just missed his wife and was feeling a bit moody. Then he might smash up a room or something.

"It wasn't a nightly occurrence, and it didn't happen in every hotel we ever went to. We stayed in a lot of hotels during 12 years and they didn't all get demolished. I don't think we ever did any damage in The New York Plaza. The worst thing that happened there was when a pool ball went through a window. Which was a bit dangerous because we were up on the 25th floor. Thank God it hit the pavement and didn't go through a car or somebody's head."

John's brother Mick presents a different slant on the drummer's reputation. "You read about him wrecking hotels, but nine times out of ten he was encouraged to do it. The hotel manager even used to help! They'd do ten grand's worth of damage and get a 40 grand bill. The band always paid, and nobody cared. In any case, John didn't break things so much as meticulously take them apart with a screwdriver. It was all paid for, and Zeppelin spent a fortune on hotels anyway. It all sounded worse when you read about it – but football yobs wreck trains every week, and they don't pay for it."

> "Zeppelin spent a fortune on hotels anyway ... Football yobs wreck trains every week, and they don't pay for it"

Another oft-repeated tale is that Bonzo rode a motorbike through the corridors of the Hyatt House in Hollywood, the famed rock'n'roll hotel known affectionately as 'The Riot House'. In fact it was Richard Cole who used the bike to get around Zeppelin's far-flung suites. "Oh I had a motor bike, yeah," says Cole. "I used to keep it in my room, because we had two or three floors – we didn't have enough suites on one of the floors, so Bonham and John Paul Jones were two floors above us. Rather than walk along the corridor I used to keep the motorbike handy and I'd drive it into the elevator and then up to their floor. Then if I wanted to go out, I'd just go downstairs in the elevator and drive it straight through the lobby. It wasn't a full sized motorcycle – it was a trials bike."

SATURDAY NIGHT & TUESDAY MORNING

When John was back home in Worcester he had plenty of other friends outside of the music business to provide companionship and good sport – and of course to go drinking with. One of his best pals was businessman David Hadley, formerly with the *Birmingham Post*, a big-band fan who ran a company selling petrol, tyres and cars in Bromsgrove. Naturally he shared John's interest in cars, and also in snooker. On one occasion he organised a star-studded snooker tournament in Birmingham, attended by such luminaries as Alex 'Hurricane' Higgins. He invited John along, together with his father Jack, who was a keen snooker fan.

"As well as the tyre business I also had a company called Sponsor Sport," Hadley explains, "and used to promote snooker and darts tournaments. I'd invite celebrities like Jasper Carrot and Arthur Askey. On this occasion I invited Robert Plant and John Bonham. I told them they had to dress in suits – it was the first time I'd ever seen Robert wearing a tie in his life.

"John wanted to meet Alex Higgins, so I introduced them and left them together in the VIP cocktail bar while I went off to take care of the tournament. Alex apparently said to John, 'Have you tried the punch? Try a couple of these.' The punch contained rum, cointreau, orange juice and God knows what else. Then John said, 'Great, but have you tried Brandy Alexanders?' So they both tried these drinks, and by the time I came back these guys were pretty much out of it.

> ## "At which point John fell backwards and crash-landed in the buffet"

"I announced that the food was about to be served, at which point John fell over backwards and crash-landed in the buffet. His lovely new suit was covered in salad. He went straight through the entire spread I had paid for. Matthew [Stanislowksi] and I had to carry John out and put him in the back of his blue Mercedes limo and escort him home. But that's what happened when you put Hurricane Higgins and Bonzo together."

John's dad was oblivious to these events. He was sitting in the front row watching the snooker. "He wasn't interested in cocktails – he was a pint-of-mild sort of bloke."

David Hadley himself wasn't always just a passive observer of these binges. One Saturday morning John rang David and said he'd got tickets for a Joni Mitchell concert at Wembley Stadium and asked if he fancied coming along. Crosby, Stills & Nash were also on the bill so it sounded like a great day out. Hadley told his wife, "I'm just popping out to see a show with John. I'll see you later."

They drove to London, arrived early and were seated in the royal box. But after a quarter-of-an-hour the bar was due to close. John said, "That's no good, we're going to be here all day." He hastily ordered a case of lagers. "And while you're at it, give us that gallon bottle of Scotch Whisky from behind the bar."

During the afternoon Bonzo and David began dispensing the whisky and were joined by visiting celebrities, including Rod Stewart. The pair later went out to dinner with Rod at a Chinese restaurant in Chelsea, followed by an after-gig party at Quaglino's, where Birmingham band Mike Sheridan & The Nightriders were playing.

David later woke up in the back of John's Range Rover, parked in a motorway service station. He literally didn't know what day it was but assumed it was Sunday. "No, it's Tuesday, old pal," John told him. David Hadley vows that to this day he still doesn't know what happened to Sunday and Monday.

ANOTHER WET DJ

All John's farming mates went to see him play with Zeppelin at Earls Court in London in 1975. They knew he was a drummer with a successful band, but had no real idea of the band's status. Says Hadley, "They probably thought it was like The Hollies or something. Zeppelin played so seldom in the UK and never issued any singles so the general public didn't realise how big they were. When Zeppelin began playing and then Bonzo did a 30-minute drum solo, they nearly fell over: 'Look at our neighbour up there!'"

Those five nights of Earls Court concerts in May 1975 were among the best Zeppelin ever performed, and were landmarks in their career. John said later: "I thought they were the best shows we ever put on in England. I always get tense before a show, and we were expecting trouble from such a huge audience. But everything went really well."

After Earls Court the band had to leave the country as tax exiles, and they took up residence in Montreux, Switzerland. It was then that a run of bad luck began which dogged Zeppelin for the next few years. Robert and Maureen Plant suffered a car crash while they were on holiday on the Greek island of Rhodes. Both were badly injured, and after treatment Robert had to be airlifted home, and then to Jersey in the Channel Islands. While the band was staying there, David Hadley was invited over from the Midlands to join Bonzo for another long weekend.

> **"I thought they were the best shows we ever put on in England"**

"Jersey was the nearest they could get to Britain while they were tax exiles, so they camped at the Atlantic Hotel for a few weeks. They said they'd do a gig for a small club owner, who had been very friendly and helpful to them. They just asked that he didn't tell anyone about it beforehand."

They turned up to play at Behan's Nightclub, Robert in a wheelchair with his leg in plaster, still recovering from the car crash. Hadley describes the scene: "So these guys shuffle on stage and the club owner says, 'Ladies and gentlemen, a special treat tonight – Led Zeppelin!' They all thought he was kidding, of course, but once the band actually started to play people ran out into the streets to round up all their friends. And there was Robert singing in a wheelchair in this little club. It was a wild few days.

"Bonzo put on a fancy-dress outfit later and drove a Bentley round the island with the police chasing him. I think he did three laps of the island but they couldn't catch him. He'd learned all these moves to outwit the police."

Once Robert had recovered sufficiently, Zeppelin went to Musicland studios in Munich, Germany in October 1975 where they recorded their next album, *Presence*, which was eventually released during April 1976. In October came the release of the movie and soundtrack album of *The Song Remains The Same*, which included a new live version of Bonham's 'Moby Dick' solo. The movie was premiered in New York and shown in London and Birmingham the following month.

> **"Bonzo put on a fancy-dress outfit and drove a Bentley round the island"**

Bonzo went to the Birmingham premiere – which led to a scene in a nightclub, as Mick Bonham recalled. "We went to the party at the Opposite Lock afterwards. Jason was there – he was only a young lad, and he got up on a drum set and was playing away to records. The DJ was set up in a box ... While Jason was playing the DJ suddenly says, 'If you think yer so good, let's hear you play this,' and puts on Sandy Nelson's 'Let There Be Drums'. Now, no one drummer can copy another drummer, so of course Jason was totally befuddled by this, and it upset him – he looked really embarrassed.

"Our John was not very happy about this at all. The DJ was kind of smirking to himself, when all of a sudden there was a loud smack! John had hit him, and he was quickly disposed of by a couple of heavy-looking blokes and thrown into the canal. It was brilliant to see this smirking face getting smacked and a big hand dragging the guy away."

BEGINNING OF THE END

Wherever they went Zeppelin made it clear they were not to be messed with. But John and his colleagues' short fuses and hands-on approach eventually caused the band some serious trouble – not least on their jinxed 11th tour of the States.

On April 1st 1977 Led Zeppelin began its biggest tour of America at the Memorial Auditorium in Dallas, Texas. They were due to play 51 dates in 30 cities, using video screens to project the band's performance at the huge venues. They'd play three-hour shows featuring some 15 songs, and then commute between cities by the 'Zeppelin Starship' (a chartered Boeing 737).

Despite bouts of illness and exhaustion, the band had their usual crazy fun on the road, until it all turned sour at a fateful concert at the Oakland Coliseum, California, on July 23rd. This was the afternoon when members of the Zeppelin entourage attacked one of promoter Bill Graham's security men, which resulted in the arrest of John Bonham, Peter Grant, Richard Cole and John Bindon, another of Zeppelin's security guards.

A row had been sparked when the security man spotted Warren Grant, Peter's seven-year-old son, attempting to take down a Led Zeppelin sign from one of the backstage trailers, as a souvenir. The guard, Jim Matzorkis, had allegedly slapped the child on the back of the head (though he later denied this, saying he'd only reprimanded the boy). John Bonham, who was taking a break from his drums during the show, claims he saw the incident, came across and kicked the guard. He then returned to the stage.

Peter Grant heard what had happened, and he and his bodyguard John Bindon found and beat up Bill Graham's man inside a trailer, while Cole kept watch outside. The guard was taken to hospital for treatment.

Bill Graham, who was also manhandled by Grant, waited until after the second show was completed on July 24th, then the following day armed police from the Sheriff's department arrested the Zeppelin men. All four were questioned, charged with battery, and then released on bail. The criminal charges were followed by a civil action, which dragged on for months.

Meanwhile the band left Oakland and flew to New Orleans, where even worse was to follow. Robert Plant was at the hotel when he was informed that his five-year-old son Karac had been taken ill with a stomach infection. The child's condition worsened,

> **"They incurred suspended prison sentences and fines of several hundred dollars"**

and an ambulance was called, but he died before reaching hospital. Plant flew home to England, and the last seven dates of the tour were cancelled. Led Zeppelin would never return to America.

In February 1978 the criminal case against Grant, Bonham, Bindon and Cole was heard in California. They incurred suspended prison sentences and fines of several hundred dollars. Although the band had got off lightly in the eyes of the promoter, the whole incident undoubtedly damaged the band's reputation in the United States, where they were heavily criticised.

That same year, on September 8th, John's friend Keith Moon died from an overdose of tablets prescribed to combat his alcoholism. The rock'n'roll gloss was fading.

LOOKING FOR TROUBLE

The effect of John's own drinking on his moods and behaviour seemed to be unpredictable. His friends all stress how likable he was when sober, and even sometimes when drunk. Carmine Appice avows that he "never, ever had a problem with Bonzo". But there are recurring stories of how quickly he could get angry with anyone who upset him.

Bev Bevan sums it up by saying: "He was an extrovert character, but unfortunately the drink just got too much for him. He just overdid it. And he wasn't the best of drunks. He was such a smashing guy when he wasn't drinking – a lovely big huggable friendly sort of bloke, but when he had too much to drink he did get quite aggressive and started picking fights. He wasn't a friendly drunk – he went the opposite way, which was a shame. I began to lose contact with him towards the end of his life. He went in with this different crowd and he began to get quite a reputation for causing trouble, which I didn't like.

> **"For every drink he bought the band and me, he had six … He had a little tray of Brandy Alexanders … within the space of an hour he may have had 24 of these things"**

"He was a bit similar to Keith Moon. They both felt they had to live up to their reputations. Keith had to do something mad, because it was what people expected. With Bonzo it was like, 'Watch how much this bloke can drink…'

"The last time I saw him was when I was with ELO and we were staying at the Hyatt House Hotel in Hollywood … Zeppelin were in town and I invited John over. There was a very good house band in the bar and I'd got up and jammed with them. They were very kind and said, 'You're a great player.' I said, 'Well thanks very much, but you should see my pal John if you want to see a drummer.' So he turned up and was being very generous, buying us all drinks. But for every drink he bought the band and me, he had six.

"I would have a brandy and Coke and he would have six brandy Alexanders. He had a little tray of them and he'd knock them back like Schnapps. So within the space of an hour he may have had 24 of these things. He then got up on stage to jam with the band. They started to play 'Superstition', the old Stevie Wonder song. I'd been telling everyone that this guy was the best drummer in the world, and of course he was terrible. He was all over the place, and he couldn't keep time. The band looked at me as if to say, 'Are you sure?' That was the last time I saw him."

THE OUT DOOR

Still in a state of shock after the Oakland assault affair, and the heartbreaking death of Plant's young son, Led Zeppelin nonetheless picked up the pieces and carried on.

In October 1978 Bonham and John Paul Jones were invited to take part in the 'Rockestra' organised by Paul McCartney, playing on a 'super session' at Abbey Road studios. Two of the tracks, 'Rockestra Theme' and 'So Glad To See You Here', were featured on the later Wings album *Back To The Egg*.

In December Zeppelin went to Abba's Polar studios in Stockholm where they began recording sessions for what turned out to be their last studio album together, *In Through The Out Door*. The album was completed in February 1979, and it was announced that Led Zeppelin would return to live performing with two shows at Knebworth on August 4th and 11th, with Keith Richard's New Barbarians supporting them on the second show. Zeppelin performed for over three hours and used video screens and laser lights, as they played their old favourites 'Stairway To Heaven', 'Rock And Roll' and 'Communication Breakdown'. It was at one of these shows that Jason Bonham surprised Jones, Page and Plant when he got up on the drums during the soundcheck and seemed to be playing pretty much as well as his father.

Although punk rock and new wave had taken hold during Zeppelin's prolonged absence, their new album went to number 1 in the album charts and sold over four million copies in the US. On December 29th Bonham, Plant and Jones appeared at the UNICEF charity concert Rock For Kampuchea at London's Hammersmith Odeon venue.

Then on June 17th 1980 Led Zeppelin embarked on their first European tour since 1973, with a show at the Westfalenhalle, Dortmund. But a show in Nuremberg on the 27th had to be stopped after three numbers when John was taken ill. He was said to be suffering from physical exhaustion. He appeared unwell for the rest of the tour.

At Munich he invited his old pal Simon Kirke, from Free and Bad Company, to sit in with the band on 'Whole Lotta Love'. Simon recalls: "Bonzo and I did a duet. We had two kits set up. He had phoned all the instrument dealers in Munich and said, 'I want a drum kit sent down, right away.'" Simon felt quite daunted at the prospect of learning the whole 12-minute piece just before show time. "It's quite a complex arrangement to 'Whole Lotta Love'. So Bonzo says to me, banging on his knees, 'Right we do this, got that? Right, then Pagey takes over, bomp, bomp. Got that? Great.'

"And it was all done on the knees in the hotel room before we went on stage. I dunno how, but I got through to the end. The only thing that upset me was I found all the cymbals were the wrong way round. But hearing those opening notes was the heaviest thing I've ever heard.

And then of course … he died just a month or so later. And yet John was fine when I saw him. The last time I saw him he was packing up little dolls he had collected from different countries for his daughter Zoe. So this image of the wild man, eating maids for breakfast, was wiped out. He was wrapping up all these little dolls… 'One from Austria, one from Switzerland…' He was such a tidy man, and his clothes were always immaculate."

Bonham talked to Zeppelin fan Dave Lewis after the European shows and told him he had enjoyed playing them. He seemed quite upbeat about the future. "Overall everyone was dead chuffed with the way the tour went," Bonzo remarked. "There were so many things that could have gone wrong. We want to keep working, and of course we want to do England."

WE TRIED TO WAKE HIM

On their return to the UK it was announced that Zeppelin would do their first North American tour since 1977, starting in Montreal, Canada on October 17th 1980. In September the band began rehearsals at Jimmy Page's house in Windsor.

It was there that tragedy struck. On the morning of September 25th, John Paul Jones and road manager Benje LeFevre found John Bonham dead in bed. He had spent the previous day drinking heavily, and had been put to bed after falling unconscious, and left to sleep it off. Police were called to the house but there were no suspicious circumstances. An inquest was held on October 8th at East Berkshire coroner's court, and it was revealed that John had died from inhalation of vomit during his sleep. He had suffered a pulmonary oedema, a swelling of blood vessels, due to excess fluid being present. The cause of death was put down to "consumption of alcohol", and a verdict of accidental death was recorded. Bonham was just 31 years old.

> **"Last time I saw him he was packing up little dolls for his daughter … this image of the wild man … was wiped out"**

It was later established that John had started a lunchtime drinking session that carried on until midnight. He had consumed some 40 measures of vodka during a 12-hour session, and after falling asleep on a sofa was put to bed by an assistant and laid on his side with pillows for support. When it was realised something was wrong the following morning, an ambulance was called, but it was already too late.

John Paul Jones: "Benje and I found him. It was like, 'Let's go up and look at Bonzo, see how he is.' We tried to wake him up ... it was terrible. Then I had to tell the other two. In fact everyone was in particularly high spirits that morning. Then I had to break the news to Jimmy and Robert. It made me feel very angry – at the waste of him.

"We had just started rehearsing for a tour of America when Bonzo died. It was just at the point where we had all come back together again. We had synchronised again and had high hopes that it was all coming right. Bonzo had been getting a bit erratic, and I can't say he was in good shape, because he wasn't. There were some good moments during the last rehearsals... but then he started on the vodka."

Some people have speculated that John was particularly nervous about returning to America, where there had been such bad feeling in 1977, and this exacerbated his drinking. But Jones says: "I think he had been drinking because there were some problems in his personal life. But he died because of an accident. He was lying down the wrong way, which could have happened to anybody who drank a lot."

> **"Everyone was in particularly high spirits that morning. Then I had to break the news to Jimmy and Robert. It made me feel angry – at the waste of him"**

Everything takes on new significance with hindsight. Robert Plant remembers John's mood as they drove to what was to be their final rehearsal together. "On the very last day of his life, as we drove to the rehearsal, he was not quite as happy as he could be. He said, 'I've had it with playing drums. Everybody plays better than me.' We were driving in the car and he pulled off the sun visor and threw it out the window as he was talking. He said, 'I'll tell you what, when we get to the rehearsal, you play the drums and I'll sing.' And that was our last rehearsal."

The group were shattered by John's death, and his family devastated. All touring plans were immediately cancelled. As the news made headlines around the world, tributes poured in from fellow drummers. The funeral took place at Rushock Parish church in Worcestershire on October 10th, and was attended by 250 mourners, including family, friends, bandmates and fellow musicians, notably Roy Wood, Denny Laine, Bev Bevan and Jeff Lynne. Among the many wreaths was one from Paul McCartney. More tributes were received from Carmine Appice, Phil Collins, Cozy Powell and Carl Palmer.

Bev Bevan recalls: "It came as such a shock when I heard the news of his death on the radio. I went to the funeral, and it was the worst I have ever been to, because he was so young and he had so much in front of him. His wife and family and relatives were utterly distraught. There was much weeping. The church was jammed and there were so many people outside. It was very, very sad. He was such a brilliant drummer – who knows what he would have done."

Simon Kirke says: "I felt very privileged to have known Bonzo. We were roughly the same age, and we were each other's fans. He was my all-time favourite drummer – he was the best. There was no one within a mile of Bonzo."

> ## "He was such a brilliant drummer – who knows what he would have done"

In the immediate aftermath of John's untimely death there was inevitable speculation that he might be replaced, and Zeppelin would carry on, as The Who had done when Keith Moon died. Among those suggested for the post were Carmine Appice and Cozy Powell.

But on December 4th 1980 an announcement from SwanSong put an end to all the rumours. A statement was issued which read: "We wish it to be known that the loss of our dear friend and the deep sense of undivided harmony felt by ourselves and our manager, have led us to decide that we could not continue as we were." Jimmy Page later amplified these remarks by saying that Led Zeppelin just could not have continued playing their old numbers without John Bonham. The glory days were over.

IN BONZO'S SHADOW

Two years after John's death, Jimmy Page paid tribute to his memory by including the track 'Bonzo's Montreux' on the final Led Zeppelin album, *Coda*, a collection of unreleased tracks and demos. The track featured the 'John Bonham Drum Orchestra', with John soloing on electronically-treated timpani as well as his trusty acoustic drums. Over the next few years Page worked on the digital remasters of Led Zeppelin's classic recordings for release on CD, so new generations could enjoy the unique sound of John Bonham's thunder of drums.

As for performing as Led Zeppelin without Bonzo, Page and Plant were both adamant at the time that they could not imagine such a thing. Indeed it was several years before Page could touch a guitar again, while Plant, devastated by the death of his close friend, opted to forge an entirely new musical career, largely away from the hard rock of the 1970s.

Eventually the pressure of public opinion, and their desperate desire to perform again, meant each staged a return to touring with their own regular bands. When Jimmy Page formed The Firm with ex-Free singer Paul Rodgers in December 1984, they fully intended to play some Zeppelin songs as well as new material. After all, during the 1980s tunes like 'Black Dog' and 'Rock And Roll' had been revived by the new wave of metallers, and there was a whole genre of Zeppelin clones, from White Lion to Kingdom Come. It was time to fight back and show who was boss.

The Firm needed a solid drummer, and they recruited Chris Slade – ex-Manfred Mann's Earthband. He'd also played with Tom Jones and Uriah Heep, and later drummed for AC/DC. Chris was the first heavyweight required to drum in the shadow of Bonham. He acquitted himself well on tour and on the band's two albums, but then The Firm broke up.

REUNION, OF SORTS

Bob Geldof pursued and finally persuaded Led Zeppelin to reform for the massive famine-relief event Live Aid in 1985. For this one-off they brought in two drummers – namely Phil Collins and Chic's Tony Thompson – to try and recreate the energy generated by the man in the bowler hat and boiler suit.

The Live Aid gig turned out to be a fraught occasion, for various reasons. The Zep boys were under-rehearsed, and it showed. If nothing else their somewhat ramshackle performance showed how much Zeppelin relied on that solid rhythmic pulse that only Bonzo could provide, despite the work of Collins and Thompson.

Collins had been a long-term fan of John Bonham. He understood John's special qualities and appreciated his importance to the Zeppelin sound, so he regarded it as a unique treat to be asked to play with them – even if it meant rushing across the Atlantic to be at the gig on time.

There were two Live Aid shows, one at Wembley, in London, and the other at the JFK Stadium in Philadelphia. Led Zeppelin appeared at the US show, playing 'Stairway To Heaven', 'Rock And Roll' and 'Whole Lotta Love'. But Collins had already agreed to sing onstage with Sting at the British event. On the day, thanks to a supersonic flight on Concorde, he managed to do both. But it wasn't the ideal circumstances for a smooth-running performance, as Phil admits. But there were other problems too, he says.

> "For Live Aid they brought in two drummers to try and recreate the energy generated by the man in the bowler hat and boiler suit"

Despite the excitement of being there, Collins wasn't happy with the gig. "Obviously they hadn't played together for years and there was a lot on the line – the Zeppelin revival. But it was funny... Tony Thompson was playing drums too and had rehearsed with Zeppelin. I couldn't rehearse because I had been on the road for five months at that point. I got together with them in the dressing room and I had the funny feeling of being the new boy. Tony is a great drummer, but when you are playing with two drummers you have to have a certain attitude – you have to back off and not have so many egos, and play as a unit. Tony didn't seem to want to do that, and within five minutes of me being on stage I felt, 'Get me out of here.'

"It was just weird. If you are playing straight time, one of the drummers can't start doing triplet fills, 'cos it will start sounding real messy. That was going on, and speeding up and slowing down. It wasn't particularly enjoyable, and because I hadn't rehearsed, and because I'd flown across the Atlantic, Robert laid a lot of the blame at my door. In fact I was trying to play as little as possible, to get out of everybody's way. He just thought I was tired. But I knew what they wanted. John Bonham was one of my favourite drummers. I grew up watching Zeppelin from their first gig at the Marquee.

> "I knew what they wanted. John Bonham was one of my all-time favourite drummers. I grew up watching Zeppelin from their first gig at the Marquee"

"[At Live Aid] 'Whole Lotta Love' was a bit chaotic, because they can rehearse until they are blue in the face, but at the given moment they will do what they want to do. Jimmy was feeding back and getting his violin bow out... it was all a bit peculiar. Nice place to visit, but I wouldn't want to live there."

THE GENES REMAIN...

After Live Aid, the band had a few more rehearsals with Tony Thompson on drums, but opted not to re-form. Page's next project was a new band with Jason Bonham on drums. Now in his 20s and playing with his own brand of attack, Jason must have known his father would have been proud and delighted that Jimmy had given him such an accolade.

But Jason's dream gig came about when he played on the second Zeppelin reunion, at the Atlantic Records birthday celebrations at Madison Square Garden in New York in May 1988. This time there was no second drummer, and Jason played with great confidence and authority, giving Plant, Page and Jones the rhythmic kick they needed. It could still never be the original Led Zeppelin, of course, but it's probably as as close as we'll ever get.

Page later remarked: "It's funny – Jason knew the Zeppelin tracks better than I did ... He remembered every note and every phrase we had played on the recorded version of things like 'The Song Remains The Same', while we remembered them from the last time we played them, on the last European tour, when we had changed them all around... John was the greatest rock drummer ever, as far as I'm concerned, and Jason was obviously taught by his father – he has the same approach to the bass drum, for example, and has the same intensity. He had the greatest teacher in the world."

> "John was the greatest rock drummer ever, as far as I'm concerned, and Jason was obviously taught by his father ... He had the greatest teacher in the world"

When Robert and Jimmy got back together again for their 1994 Page & Plant tour, they hired as their drummer the young, good-looking Michael Lee, formerly of Little Angels and The Cult. Lee impressed everyone with his dynamic playing. It seemed the younger the drummer, the stronger the spirit of Bonham prevailed.

You can't help wondering if Bonzo would have been impressed by all the admirers who have attempted to follow in his footsteps. More than likely he would have been flattered. But if by some divine intervention he could have seen this army of 'dep' drummers paying such heartfelt tribute, you suspect he might simply have let out a mighty cry of: "Shut up, you buggers!"

Postscript: Michael Bonham, John's younger brother, and supplier of many anecdotes and reminiscences for this book, died on January 14th 2000 after suffering a heart attack, aged only 49. He had also been writing his own personal account of the life of his brother, whom he so much admired and missed. John and Michael's sister Debbie intends that Michael's completed book will still be published, and should certainly be bought and read by all fans of John Henry Bonham.

ROCK AND ROLL

CHAPTER 5

John was the greatest rock drummer
ever, as far as I'm concerned.

JIMMY PAGE

So just how good, and influential, was John Bonham's drumming style?
In this section Geoff Nicholls analyses Bonzo the player...

Two decades after his death, Bonham's name still crops up in
almost every interview with a contemporary rock drummer. When
Rhythm magazine's readers voted for 'most influential drummers
of the 20th century', he came second only to Buddy Rich.

One thing's for sure. John Bonham could not have sustained the level of respect afforded to him if it weren't for the fact he was extraordinarily good. But it's more than just ability that makes other drummers love him.

Bonham's technique was certainly way above average for an un-tutored British rock drummer of the late 1960s. There were, of course, many drummers in the US who had received serious tuition and were technically more knowledgeable – including the likes of Carmine Appice. And during this period and into the early 1970s a new generation of studious, assured British rock drummers emerged alongside Bonham, such as Carl Palmer, Jon Hiseman and Bill Bruford.

But if Bonzo lacked something in schooling compared with this new breed, he made up for it with sheer talent, bravado and vision. No one had his combination of sound, power, feel and drama.

John Bonham was a self-taught drummer. This was not as unusual as it might seem today. Back in the mid 1960s rock was an emerging, evolving music – no one could 'teach' you how to play it, because it was still being invented. You picked it up as you went along and did your own thing. Like most other drummers at the time, John learned by listening to records and experimenting.

There were traditional drum teachers around who could show you how to play rumbas and quick-steps, and even those who might unravel the intricacies of bebop, big-band jazz and orchestral percussion. But there really wasn't anyone who could have helped Bonzo develop the power he was looking for.

Still, there's plenty of evidence that Bonham was a voracious student of the drums. He was aware of the more sophisticated jazz drummers of the time, both British and American. As we've seen, John sought out local jazz drummer Garry Allcock, who passed on a few pointers. "I remember talking to him about Joe Morello," says Allcock, "and also at great length about Kenny Clare and Phil Seamen." Seamen was the great British bebop drummer who gave lessons to Ginger Baker, but died young after years of drug addiction. "Phil would go out on a limb and one night play like Buddy Rich, and the next be so crap it wasn't true. Mainly because of the stuff he was on, I suppose. And I remember saying to John, 'If you're gonna go, really go for it, and it will either come off or not.' And he agreed. He had that attitude."

The young Bonham occasionally admired pop-group drummers, particularly Bobby Elliott of The Hollies, whom Bonzo's mate Mac Poole describes as *the* 1960s drummer. "Bobby had a style all his own," says Poole. "He's an unsung hero." But by 1965 Keith Moon had transformed orderly 'beat group' drumming into the wildest extemporised rock imaginable, and the following year Ginger Baker had assumed Moon's savage mantle. Baker had a reputation as the most ear-shattering drummer around, at the same time adding a dimension of technical control.

Bonham was impressed by Baker's skill, and was determined to become the next important rock drummer – the loudest, the most dynamic, the best. When he met Carmine Appice in 1968, he already had the platform and the attitude. Appice provided the final affirmation, if it were needed, that Bonham was on the right path, and the American also helped to advance Bonzo's technical skills, whether directly or not.

We'll break down Bonham's playing into three areas for examination: Volume, Sound, and Technique. After that, we'll have a look through Bonzo's drum kits and hardware.

VOLUME

Deep Purple's Ian Paice remembers the first time he saw John play, in pre-Led Zeppelin days, backing US folk singer Tim Rose in a London club. "Everything was going along quite sweetly for the first couple of songs, which were basically acoustic," says Paice. "Then all hell broke loose. John played beautifully, but he played the same way he did in Zeppelin. So from this mellow little folky music it became 'drums with inaudible musical accompaniment'. Gloriously hilarious!"

Much has been made of the fact that Bonham was loud. Indeed, stories like this only add to the image. But Bonham – like Ginger Baker before him – was probably only loud in relation to what was going on during the time he emerged. He may have been a bit over-powering in an acoustic setting, but as serious amplification started to evolve in the late 1960s drummers had no option but to play louder. Today, many rock drummers play that loud – with many hard-rock and heavy-metal players considerably louder.

More important than simple volume, though, was the way in which Bonham revealed the future of stadium-rock 'attitude', creating a template which has survived to this day. He showed how to play 'big', using broad strokes on a large canvas.

Elton John's long-time drummer Charlie Morgan, who knows a thing or two about stadium playing, exclaims, "Bonzo! Now, there was a totally committed player. I think his biggest character trait was attitude. Pure balls-out, head-down 'tood."

Bassist Dave Pegg still holds that Bonham was "the loudest drummer I've ever heard in my life". But he explains what made it more than just a decibel-busting racket. "It wasn't a 'noise', because the kit was tuned incredibly well. The bass drum sound was so different from anyone else's." Zep tour manager Richard Cole puts it simply: "He had *the* most powerful sound – the sound every drummer has been trying to get ever since."

SOUND

To understand why Bonham's sound was so remarkable, it should be remembered that throughout the 1970s – while all around him were removing the bottom heads from their drums, plastering their top heads with sticky tape and stuffing their bass drums with pillows – Bonham played massive drums with both heads intact, and no damping. His expansive tone flew in the face of the 1970s 'cardboard box' sound. This in itself took great strength of character.

Most drummers and engineers went the 'cardboard' route largely because the 1970s was the decade when close-miking of individual drums was developed. Players and studio personnel alike soon found out that most rock drum kits didn't stand up to such close scrutiny, as the drums had mostly been tuned only haphazardly for live work.

Placing a microphone an inch from the top head of each drum revealed all manner of embarrassing rings and hums. By removing the bottom head and taping the top head, the offending overtones were smothered. But this was a short-term gain. The result was certainly clean signals – and crappy drum sounds. Bonham would have none of this, and he found an ally in guitarist/producer Jimmy Page, who had seen drums suffer from this indignity in studios during his session career.

Dave Mattacks, world-respected freelance drummer and good friend of Bonham, says: "The big misconception is that you have to hit hard to get John's sound. It most definitely helps, but that's not why he sounded like that. There are guys out there now who hit as hard or harder, but don't know how to tune to get that sound.

"It was a combination of hard playing and tuning. John adopted a variation on a [live] big-band type of tuning – big drums with high 'jazz' tuning, wide open with no damping. Kits tuned that way don't sound quite so good in small rooms and close-miked. You have to get the mikes away from the drums to 'hear' the full sound properly – hence the contemporary love affair with large rooms and ambient mikes. But it's essential for the kit to be balanced with itself for this to work, for instance so the cymbals don't overpower the drums." This was presumably the cause of the problems Bonzo experienced early in his career when he was told by one studio engineer that his drums were "unrecordable".

In the days before miking, drummers would tune drums high to project better – because the perceived pitch of a drum drops considerably over a short distance. With the advent of close-miking on-stage and in the studio, the tuning of drums became deeper. Ringo Starr had already pioneered deep and damped tuning on The Beatles' later albums, partly because the group had stopped live touring and were experimenting with close-miking and multi-track recording.

Unfortunately the incredible sounds that The Beatles and their studio team achieved were not mirrored in the recordings of the average drummer. Drum sounds in the 1970s were regularly an abomination. But not Bonzo's. As Dave Mattacks said, Bonzo used big drums and tuned them up high. A large drum will give a naturally broader and deeper sound anyway, so if you tune it high you get the best of both worlds: real depth and maximum projection.

Well-known California drum maker Jeff Ocheltree met Bonham in 1975 and became his drum-tech on tour in 1977 and 1979. Previously, Ocheltree had pioneered the modern drum-tech's role while working with fusion genius Billy Cobham. Ocheltree says a major factor in Bonham's sound was that the Zep drummer paid attention to bottom-head tuning, something most rock drummers neglected.

"With the toms, he tuned the bottom head higher than the top head," says Ocheltree. "The batter [top] head forces the air to the bottom head to create the sound, so if you have a loose bottom head you get a real mid-to-low-end sound. He didn't want that – he wanted the drum to speak, like Cobham. He was one of the few drummers in rock who did that.

"In the studio he tuned the bottom heads higher than he did live. The 14 or 15-inch shell-mount tom was similar in pitch to the 16in floor tom, except the bottom head was tuned up really high, like a 10 or 12in would be today. Yet the way he hit the drum, and with the type of head he used, it cut through and had more warmth."

Ocheltree says Bonham's snare drum had a Remo Emperor or Ludwig coated batter "cranked up quite high". The bass drum was also tuned up high – and had both heads intact. "Nobody who knew about drums would cut a hole in the front head back then, it was unheard of. He tuned the bass drum way up, a lot higher than you'd think. There was no damping at all, no felt strips. In the big room, he wanted to be more present in the mix. He knew from the get-go that if you give them more than they need they have less to screw with."

Dave Mattacks remembers that Bonham's stainless steel kit had the bass drum "tuned like his top tom", and the snare drum was wide open and really tight. But in spite of the obvious care Bonzo took over his tuning, the most astonishing thing, Mattacks recalls, is that Bonham retained 'his' sound, whatever kit he happened to be playing – even a miniature one. Bass-playing colleague Dave Pegg backs this up: "Bonzo was incredible. His drum sound never changed – it was like that from the word go."

Led Zeppelin tour manager Richard Cole underlines the undisputed fact that Jimmy Page was the producer. "So you can't really credit anybody else for getting that sound. Obviously Bonham would move the drums around to see if they'd sound better, and he'd record in different houses, like Headley Grange and Stargroves. But Pagey was the producer and knew exactly what he wanted."

Drummer Ian Paice recalls Bonham admitting to him that a lot of the studio sound came from Jimmy Page and engineer Glyn Johns. Paice makes a fundamental point when he says: "To my mind it's the way you hit 'em that counts." Mentioning 'When The Levee Breaks' as an example, Paice says that without John doing what he did, the sound heard on record could never have been made.

TECHNIQUE

John Paul Jones got closer than anyone to Bonham in full flight. He says: "He used to hit hard and he was loud, but he was actually a very subtle drummer in a lot of ways. He never played the same thing twice and there was always a lot going on in his playing. There was light and shade, colour and groove."

Bonzo's first drum roadie Glen Colson was another close-up admirer. "He looked like a big clumsy guy, but he was incredibly strong. He was absolutely sensational, and fearless. Kenny [Pickett, road manager] used to say to me, 'Watch him, he's completely mad!'"

Bonham certainly wasn't afraid to try out different techniques or playing styles, irrespective of where he'd picked them up. "He'd take a drum break right into the verse of a tune, which is a kind of a rock'n'roll thing," Colson recalls. "You'd hear that on a few old Jerry Lee Lewis records, and it became a style thing. The drummer would keep a roll going right into a verse – he didn't stop and go back to the snare drum, he'd keep on rolling right round the kit. So John used to go into these really long rolls, which started way before they should and end way longer. You can hear him doing it on the early Zeppelin records."

To be picky, Bonham's overall drumming technique might be viewed as slightly unorthodox. He played backbeats with his left hand thumb up, timpani style, while he preferred to use his right hand palm-over, 'German' side-drum style, and with the fulcrum slightly higher up the stick. But when it came to playing single-stroke rolls on the snare or around the kit there was no unevenness. In fact quite the contrary: his confidence in execution was one of his most impressive strengths.

Although he looks powerful, and it may seem that he's relying on his forearms, closer inspection reveals he had flexible wrists and a light grip, which gave him the stamina to play with consistency throughout epic shows.

But it was John's bass drum playing which, everyone agrees, was the highlight of his drumming style – for instance, slipping in the last two beats of a 16th-note triplet between snare and hi-hat, which was influenced, unwittingly, by Carmine Appice. Whatever the sources, he made these tricks his own, and revelled in showing them off whenever possible. Even an astounded Jimi Hendrix commented to Robert Plant after a gig one night, "That drummer of yours has a right foot like a pair of castanets."

Glen Colson recalls being fascinated watching Bonzo's footwork from the edge of the stage. "He could play better bass drum than Buddy Rich or Joe Morello. Every time he hit the drum it was a double beat. All he used was a Ludwig SpeedKing pedal, which he played with the ball of his foot."

Many heavy-footed rockers slam the bass drum and dig the pedal beater into the head. But the act of lifting the heel for extra power encourages the player to rest the beater against the head between strokes. Because Bonham's bass drum was tuned high with no damping it seems unlikely this method would have worked for him. He had to glance the beater off the head. Otherwise there would have been a muffled, multi-beat 'boinging' effect. Dave Mattacks says Bonham obviously developed this way of playing early on.

His posture, for a relatively big guy, was exemplary and he looked comfortable playing. Glen Colson remarks: "He sat really low at the drum kit, and I couldn't work out how he could play from down there."

Many of his predecessors, from Buddy Rich to Ringo Starr and Bobby Elliott, sat high above their drums, but Bonzo obviously found that sitting with his thighs extending at almost perfect right angles to his torso gave him the power and control he needed.

Those tricky bass drum moves can only come about through a relaxed control, and not through brute strength. This in itself negates the idea of Bonham as a crude basher. He was a master of his instrument, who knew exactly how to draw the maximum sound out of his highly sensitive drums, and we'll discuss this on the next few pages.

BONZO'S INFLUENCE

John Bonham certainly knew his craft, though the extraordinary esteem in which he is held by drummers today must also be seen in the context of Led Zeppelin as the ultimate rock band. Zeppelin encapsulate the bare-chested, preening, slim-hipped, long-haired ideal of the bad-boy, sex-obsessed rock group. They epitomise the adolescent fantasy of what a cool-nasty rock band should be – a stereotype which has long since become a cliché. Inevitably they are held responsible for the thousands of dreadful poodle-haired imitators they inspired.

Yet musically Zeppelin themselves were much greater and broader in ambition than this. And John Bonham had many more strings to his bow than heavy metal. In Chapter

Six we'll examine some of the tracks from Zeppelin's original studio recordings which illustrate the wide scope of Bonzo's abilities and influence.

Before that, we'll have a look in some detail at the drum kits and percussion equipment Bonham used during his entire playing career, and how these may have affected his performances, on-stage or in the studio, and ultimately contributed to the Bonham sound and legend. We'll also try to trace what's become of this gear since.

JOHN BONHAM'S DRUMS

Bonzo was a Ludwig enthusiast throughout his career. In his early bands, A Way Of Life and Band Of Joy, he played a four-piece Ludwig kit in Sparkle Green (Ludwig finish number 2004). The kit was a Super Classic: 22in x14in bass drum, 13x9 and 16x16 tom toms, with a 14x5in Supraphonic 400 metal-shell snare drum. This had been the standard rock drum kit in Britain, for those who could afford one, since Ringo Starr had swapped to Ludwig from the British brand Premier in 1963.

Ludwig drums were significantly more expensive to buy than the home-grown brand, but were considered better sounding and louder than Premier, important considerations at a time when miking up was still in its infancy. The thin three-ply mahogany/poplar/mahogany shells, with their interior coat of white paint, were brighter and more resonant than Premier's. And American Ludwig or Remo heads were generally considered – rightly or wrongly – as better than Premier's Everplay Extra heads.

Bass guitarist Dave Pegg says that when he played with John in the group A Way Of Life, the drummer already had a Ludwig kit. "It sounded absolutely huge," recalls Pegg. "It wasn't a huge kit, but it was phenomenally loud."

By mid 1968, Bonham was touring with American folk singer Tim Rose and playing the same green-glitter Super Classic. The set was eventually bought by British drummer Robin Melville, who lives in Cumbria. "There was a heavy four-piece band in the Cumbria area led by guitarist Francis Dunnery," Melville explains. "The drummer, Frank Hall, got friendly with Bonham, and Bonham gave him the kit he used with Tim Rose. It came to me for about £40 in the late 1970s. It had 22in, 13in and 16in drums. The small tom was chipped right through to the wood where the snare drum had hit it, and the front hoop was missing off the bass drum because Frank played it without bottom heads. [Drum maker] Eddie Ryan got me a front hoop and I got some new tension rods. There was no snare drum. I couldn't see any date stamps inside because it was pretty dirty. It had the original Ludwig rail consolette and cymbal arm holder."

Unfortunately the kit was so knocked about that Melville got it recovered in black by

Eddie Ryan. Melville sold it to John Andrews at the Johnny Roadhouse music shop in Manchester around 1988/9. "I got £180 for the kit, and I believe they sold it to The Verve," says Melville.

Bonham was most likely still playing this kit when he joined Led Zeppelin. From December 1968 through to the spring of 1969 Zeppelin toured the US, where Bonham shared the stage on some gigs with kindred spirit Carmine Appice of Vanilla Fudge. Appice was playing a most unusual outsized Ludwig and, as we've heard already, was so impressed by Bonzo he persuaded Ludwig to fix up John with a duplicate kit. Carmine's Ludwig had two 26in bass drums, at a time when the norm was a single 22in or, exceptionally, 24in.

Large-diameter bass drums were hardly new. Big-band drummers in the 1930s played 28in diameter drums, relics of the marching band origins of bass drums. Buddy Rich played a 24in throughout the 1960s and admitted, late in his career, to favouring his earlier 26in. And Louie Bellson had played a Gretsch double-bass-drum kit with two 20x20in monsters in 1946 with the Duke Ellington orchestra. In Britain, jazz drummer Eric Delaney soon copied Bellson, while rocker Bobby Woodman played double kicks in the early 1960s, years before Keith Moon.

But through the 1950s and 1960s the average bass-drum size had decreased, initially as a result of the influence of small-group bebop. Appice re-introduced oversize drums in order to combat the evolving power of amplification, before drummers were adequately miked. He got his Ludwig endorsement in 1968 and promptly ordered two 26x14in bass drums, a 15x12in marching tenor for his 'small' tom, an 18x16in floor tom and a 22in bass drum adapted with metal rims to serve as a second, monster floor tom. Carmine also claims this was the first Ludwig kit in maple ply. (Interestingly, maple does not appear in the Ludwig catalogues until 1974, though maple finish is available as a special order. Ringo Starr also had a maple kit around the same time as Appice and Bonham – see the Beatles' film *Let It Be*, and also the book *Beatles Gear*.)

Looking back, it's difficult to see how Bonham's technique of weaving 16th-note and broken triplet eighth-note bass drum beats between snare and hi-hat grooves would have benefited from having double kick drums. But you can bet he gave it a go – at least until his bandmates complained.

The format that Bonzo settled on – a large bass drum with one mounted tom and two floor toms – is the classic set-up of Buddy Rich and other big-band greats. Bonham even favoured the bass-drum-mounted ride cymbal and the two horizontally-mounted crashes which were so characteristic of Rich's set-up.

In the end, Bonzo's kit follows the Rich/Krupa tradition while, significantly, it was Appice's oversized double-kick set which became the model for heavy metal. You can see Appice's kit today at the Guitar & Drum Center in Los Angeles, as part of the Hollywood Rock Walk Museum. Bonzo's kit is today safely in the hands of yet another true fan, ex-Roxy Music drummer Paul Thompson.

THE MAPLE KIT: 1969–1970

Paul Thompson says, "The kit I have is a Ludwig maple finish with two 26in bass drums, plus 13in, 14in, 16in and 18in toms. I believe he got the kit just before the second album and so would have recorded 'Whole Lotta Love' and 'Moby Dick' with it. I bought the kit off a drummer friend, Colin Fairley, who used to go out with John's sister. He was visiting our hero at home, spotted the kit and asked if he wanted to sell it. Bonzo said, 'How much have you got on you?' A fiver, was the answer – so the deal took place. I bought the kit around 1976 for about £600. I saw Bonzo at the premiere for *The Song Remains The Same* [1976] and told him I had it. I think he wished he had never parted with it.

"The shells have reinforcing rings but no white paint inside," continues Thompson. "The Rogers [Swiv-O-Matic] tom mount plates are original, the actual bracket is not [see photo on page 36]. But you can see this on some of the later pictures of Bonzo with the kit. Before then he used a snare stand for the small tom tom. The cymbal mount is the original Ludwig. I got no hardware with the kit. The spurs are the original straight type – Ludwig used to put them on their bigger bass drums, usually in two pairs."

During 1969 Bonham played this kit as a four-piece, with the small tom mounted on a snare drum stand and the single 18in floor tom. In footage from the Paris TV show *Tous En Scene* (October 10th 1969) Bonzo also has a gong, but no other percussion. Presumably the scaled-down set-ups were for brief TV appearances. At the Albert Hall on June 29th that year Bonham had an extra floor tom, a gong and congas.

BACK TO GREEN SPARKLE: 1970–73

As Zeppelin toured throughout 1970, Bonzo reverted to green sparkle kits. Presumably this finish was more in keeping with John's showmanship and the spirit of the early 1970s. Tasteful natural-maple finishes would not actually become fashionable among drummers until the conservative late 1980s. At the Bath Festival (June 28th 1970) Bonzo is pictured on a green kit, now in big sizes similar to the maple kit. This set-up would become synonymous with the Bonham style and sound: 26x14in bass drum, 14x10 (later 15x12) mounted tom, 16in and 18in floor toms and a 14x6½in metal Supraphonic 402 snare drum. Jeff Ocheltree, John's US drum-tech, says that following on from the natural maple kit, John had three green sparkle kits, and that he used them on about four albums – presumably *Led Zeppelin III*, *IV*, *Houses Of The Holy*, and *Physical Graffiti*. "Pat Bonham [John's widow] has the 1971 kit, which was used on the recording of the fourth album and the 1971 tour. It has recently been loaned by Pat for display at the Rock & Roll Hall Of Fame in Cleveland, Ohio. Another kit is now owned by a collector in upstate New York."

THE AMBER VISTALITE: 1973–75

Amplification increased dramatically in the early 1970s, but close-miking was still crude, and so drummers found themselves in the ironic situation of being unable to make themselves heard. One solution was to make drums louder by utilising hard synthetic materials, and in 1973 Ludwig launched its range of multi-coloured Plexiglas-shelled Vistalite kits. Bonham's Amber Vistalite, with the 'three rings' symbol on the front bass drum head (which he'd actually featured since opening the fourth British tour in Newcastle on November 11th 1971) is perhaps his most distinctive kit, and the one he plays in *The Song Remains The Same*.

This kit fulfils Bonzo's desire to be noticed, and also reflects the early-1970s obsession with everything plastic. Hard, reflective Plexiglas surfaces made for a loud, resonant kit, if a little dry-sounding. The sound of a drum kit stems largely from the heads and from the way the player tensions those heads and strikes them. The average listener at a concert is not likely to discern much difference between a wooden kit and a set made from plastic. But in the recording studio it's a different matter – and Jeff Ocheltree believes Bonzo only ever recorded with wood-shell kits.

The Amber Vistalite kit followed the usual configuration of 26x14, 14x10, 16x16 and 18x16. But, says Ocheltree, "There were other pieces to the Amber kit which he rarely used, like 20in and 22in floor toms and an extra kick drum." During the three-night recording of *The Song Remains The Same*, however, Bonham swapped his floor tom toms between the 16in, 18in and 20in.

The plastic Vistalites have a reputation for cracking, and Ocheltree remembers holes being drilled out when the bass drum cracked, as well as the addition of bigger washers.

The Amber kit was auctioned in London, England, and bought by a collector, Bill Townsend, who took it back home to North Carolina.

SILVER GLITTER: 1975–80

Somewhere around 1975 Bonham got another Ludwig kit, this time in Sparkle Silver, and in 26in, 15in, 16in and 18in sizes. Ocheltree says, "The reason he went to the 15in (mounted) tom was because of his health. He was a little slower and he was going more to the bigger rack-mounted tom than he was the floor toms. It makes me sad to say that, but it's what I saw. He gained weight and didn't feel well. But still he never did a gig where he didn't play well. He really believed in performance."

STAINLESS STEEL: 1977–80

From 1977 Bonham acquired a stainless steel-shelled Ludwig, which became his final stage kit, featuring on the *Presence* and *In Through The Out Door* tours. This kit has the full-length tension lugs, different from all the other Bonham Ludwig kits. This would have been an exceptionally loud kit, and it can be seen for example on the 1979 Knebworth concert footage.

Jeff Ocheltree knows of only one stainless-steel kit. According to Jeff, this kit is now in the possession of another collector, name unknown, apparently an older man, in his late 60s, in Canada.

OTHER DRUM KITS OWNED BY JOHN BONHAM

GRETSCH

Besides Ludwig, American Gretsch drums were also highly regarded by rock drummers in the early 1970s, and Jeff Ocheltree believes Bonham had a couple of Gretsch kits. One was given to Traffic drummer Jim Capaldi. "It was a small one," says Ocheltree, "and Capaldi left it at a shop in London. The shop closed down and he never found it again."

CANDY STRIPE VISTALITE

Todd Trent of Ludwig says Bonham was sent 15 Vistalite drums in 1975. These were presumably in addition to the Amber Vistalites which Bonham had already been playing for some time by then. In the summer of 1975, as you'll have read in Chapter Three, Bonzo gave Chris Welch a unique black-and-white striped Vistalite kit, presumably part of this batch. The kit included typical Bonham sizes, with an extra 20in floor tom. Chris played the kit himself on jazz and rock gigs for many years. But in 1998 Chris sold the kit to an acquaintance, Phil Harris, who paid £950 for it. Harris runs a hire company and Chris was under the impression the kit would be hired out to selected local rock bands, a fate he felt would please Bonzo. However Chris was later alerted to a picture of the Vistalite in *The Sun* newspaper with the story that Mick Fleetwood had now acquired the kit and it was to be auctioned.

MIDNIGHT BLUE HAYMAN

In 1968 British Hayman drums were launched in an attempt to stem the flood of imported American drums to the UK. Many top British drummers tried out Hayman, and it seems John Bonham received a Midnight Blue Hayman kit. Certainly he had a snare drum, and this ended up in the possession of Mick Hinton, Bonham's long-time roadie. Hinton then passed the snare drum on to drummer Will Wright, who in turn left it in the hire stock of John Henry Enterprises in north London, where today it is looked after by Baz Ward. (John Henry's is a famous rehearsal and hire facility run by one John Henry – no connection to John Henry Bonham! – with whom Will Wright once played drums in a band.)

MINI KITS

Ludwig also supplied Bonzo with mini-kits for his son Jason, who showed huge promise as a drummer from an astonishingly young age (in *The Song Remains The Same* he can be seen on a mini Vistalite playing licks and twirling his sticks in exactly the same manner as his dad). Ocheltree remembers a picture that Bonzo's brother Mick took of John playing a small black-and-white Vistalite kit (with Zildjian hi-hats and Paiste ride). And he also remembers a tiny stainless steel kit that Bonzo gave to Robert Plant's son.

SNARE DRUMS

Bonham invariably played Ludwig Supraphonic 14in x 6½in 402 snare drums on stage. These drums are mostly chrome-plated over a 'Ludalloy' shell. According to Ocheltree, Bonham didn't like the more highly-prized brass-shelled drums. "He said they were too dark. Bonzo's were zinc – we used to scratch the inside to check. Bonzo said the brass ones were too 'muddy'. He said, 'I can't get the clarity, however high I tune them.'" But Ocheltree suggests that Bonham might have used a brass-shelled Black Beauty snare in the studio on a couple of occasions. As for the actual snare wires beneath the drum, which normally have 20 coils, Ocheltree reports that Bonham used a 42-strand snare on the last tour for "a little wider sound".

HEADS

Early on, Bonham used white-coated Remo or Ludwig drum heads. For the see-through Vistalite he used Remo CS (Controlled Sound) 'black dot' transparent heads. These are still single-ply but have a reinforcing circle in the centre. He also used the Ludwig equivalent 'silver dot' heads. Jeff Ocheltree says, "We went from black dots to Emperor-coated [double-ply heads] – and that was a different sound. On the Vistalite he used the black dots because you could see through them."

Ocheltree also remembers that Bonzo wouldn't change the heads unless it was absolutely necessary – he liked the sound of the heads played-in. "A couple of times I changed them without telling him," he says. "John was so against it I would take sandpaper or whatever and get them a little dirty. I worked really hard to get the stress out of the [head] collars and get the kit to sound so great that when he sat down it almost blew his mind."

CYMBALS AND GONGS

As with drum kits, the cymbals to aspire to in early-1960s Britain were American-made. Avedis Zildjians had long been the choice of professional drummers. But in the mid 1960s the Swiss-German company Paiste revolutionised the cymbal market by producing a type of cymbal aimed specifically at the amplified rock market.

Known as Giant Beats, they used a bronze alloy (B8) with a smaller tin content than (B20) Zildjians, the idea being that the sound would be more cutting and the cymbals less likely to crack. British rock drummers lapped them up.

In 1971 Paiste changed the Giant Beats to the similar 2002 series and Bonham played these for the rest of his career. His usual set-up included 24in ride, 15in Sound Edge hi-hats, 16in or 18in crash on his left, and 18in medium ride, for crashing, on his right.

At various times he doubled up with an 18in crash on his left side and a large crash/ride 20in or even 22in on his right side. And often there would be a 'ching ring' – a headless tambourine – mounted on top of the hi-hat.

Bonham also had a 36in or 38in Paiste symphonic gong behind him on stage. Ocheltree says: "There were three gongs I definitely know about. The first Paiste gongs had Chinese caricature letters on them. Later on they had 'Paiste' on them.

"John knew how to 'warm up' the gong with a mallet – and he used it for definite dynamic effect in a couple of tunes, not just for bashing. I also have a picture from Mick Bonham around 1973/75 where John has a smaller gong, maybe 22in."

TIMPANI

From 1972 Bonham also used a pair of Ludwig timpani on stage. The Ludwig 1973 catalogue describes these instruments as the Ludwig Universal Model copper-shelled timpani, available in sizes from 20in to 32in. The Universal model timps were the old-fashioned model dating back to William F Ludwig Snr's original 1919 prototype. They were designed to be portable with detachable base sections. The heads are tuned using the 'T' handles, while pitch changes and glissandi are deployed with the footpedal.

PERCUSSION

In the earlier pre-timpani days Bonham would have a pair of timbales or Natal congas on stage. There would also be a cowbell mounted on the bass drum hoop. Timps took over from congas by 1972, initially for use on 'The Rain Song' from *Physical Graffiti*.

HARDWARE

Most 1960s drum-kit hardware was not designed to withstand the onslaught of the new breed of rock drummer. Bonham found Ludwig's hi-hat pedal too flimsy and changed to the better Rogers model. Similarly the maple Ludwig kit was fitted with a Rogers Swiv-O-Matic tom holder – a common modification made by 1960s drummers including Baker and Moon. But Bonham stuck with the highly-regarded Ludwig SpeedKing bass drum pedal, usually with a felt beater, though he later used wood. The over-sized 24in ride cymbal was always mounted on a simple hinged bass drum cymbal arm in the style of Buddy Rich and earlier players. Considering Bonham's muscle this was a seemingly precarious practice – nowadays such a cymbal would be mounted on a double-braced floor stand the size of an oil rig. Still, it obviously didn't worry Bonham, nor Rich before him. Ocheltree says it was just an ordinary cymbal holder with the standard wing nut. "We kept replacing the actual holder but I never saw the cymbal fall over," he says. "Other things did break occasionally, like hi-hat clutches and timpani pedals."

STICKS

Glen Colson says that in the early days Bonham would use heavy sticks and get through three pairs a night. On later tours Jeff Ocheltree remembers him having medium-weight sticks made from hickory. "He didn't play heavy sticks, he didn't play butt-ends out, and he didn't smash the drums. He had incredible technique. He knew it wasn't about how hard you hit them, but *how* you hit them."

MICROPHONES

Ocheltree says that the Showco concert-sound company miked-up both the Vistalite and stainless steel kit using Shure Professional Series SM57 microphones. These were used for everything including the timpani and bass drum. The bass drum was miked from both the front and the batter side, near the beater.

For much of the mid-to-later period information I'm indebted to Jeff Ocheltree, who worked as Bonham's drum tech in 1977 and 1979.

HATS OFF TO BONZO

CHAPTER 6

An inspiration is what you are to me,

Inspiration – look ... see.

JIMMY PAGE / ROBERT PLANT, 'THANK YOU', *LED ZEPPELIN II*

In this section Geoff Nicholls examines Bonham's drumming on over 40 selected tracks from Zeppelin's nine studio albums. We haven't analysed every single piece the band released – we also haven't covered bootlegs, or John's earlier groups – but the chosen tracks more than adequately illustrate Bonzo's talent. Comprehensive Led Zeppelin album listings are also included.

1 9 6 9

LED ZEPPELIN

ATLANTIC 588 171 (US: SD8216)

RELEASED: **JANUARY 1969**

PRODUCED BY: **JIMMY PAGE**

ENGINEERED BY: **GLYN JOHNS**

RECORDED AND MIXED: **OCTOBER 1968 AT**

OLYMPIC STUDIO, LONDON, ENGLAND

TABLA HAND-DRUMS ON 'BLACK MOUNTAIN SIDE':

VIRAM JASANI

*Recorded in just 30 hours, during nine days in the studio, **Led Zeppelin I**, as it became known, was more or less an 'as-live' taping of the set the band performed on their first gigs in Scandinavia in the autumn of 1968, with minimal overdubbing of extra parts. The band had been together for less than three weeks, but Jimmy Page was so clear about what he wanted to achieve, and they were each so musically accomplished, that the result was a remarkably coherent, as well as ground-breaking mix of rock, blues and acoustic music. With eyes clearly on the huge American market, it was released there several weeks earlier than in the UK.*

THE TRACKS

GOOD TIMES BAD TIMES
(Page/Jones/Bonham)

running time 2.46

BABE I'M GONNA LEAVE YOU
(Page/Plant/Anne Bredon)

6.41

YOU SHOOK ME
(Willie Dixon/JB Lenoir)

6.28

DAZED AND CONFUSED
(Page)

6.26

YOUR TIME IS GONNA COME
(Page/Jones)

4.14

BLACK MOUNTAIN SIDE
(Page)

2.05

COMMUNICATION BREAKDOWN
(Page/Jones/Bonham)

2.27

I CAN'T QUIT YOU BABY
(Willie Dixon)

4.42

HOW MANY MORE TIMES
(Page/Jones/Bonham)

8.28

GOOD TIMES BAD TIMES

The astounding bass drum control, the musical tom toms, the massive sound and beautiful tuning, the atmospheric pulsing hi-hat and exploding cymbal crashes... they're all here. Although Bonham would have another decade of recording, the fact remains that here on the very first Zeppelin track he displays – fully developed – most of the features which would make his reputation. 'Good Times' is one of the all-time great opening salvos by any drummer. Bonham's playing is masterly, inventive and stacked with the 'jaw-dropping' factor.

Opening with playful hi-hat and cowbell, you await the big entrance, which soon arrives with a neat triplet fill around the kit. Immediately, the power of Bonzo's sound is right there. But nothing prepares you for what comes next. The verse rhythm is the funkiest, most daringly syncopated pattern ever heard in heavy rock. The famous three stuttering bass-drum 16ths, followed by the trademark 16th-note broken triplets, are here to freak out every drummer and send them back to their practice rooms.

And there's more. The middle section, starting at 0.57, introduces us to a second marvellously inventive pattern, this time involving a stabbing tom routine punctuating the vocal middle-eight. Bonham could have taken a much more standard approach to 'Good Times'. Instead he turned it into a grandstand showcase of his talents, lifting the track into the realms of rock genius. And the fact that it made the opening cut of the band's first album demonstrates how important the drummer was to the band.

In drumming folklore, 'Good Times' ranks alongside Zigaboo Modeliste's 'Cissy Strut', Clyde Stubblefield's 'The Funky Drummer' and David Garibaldi's 'Squib Cakes'. These are brilliantly idiosyncratic statements that tempt every serious drummer at some time to emulate them – and inevitably to fall short of the originals.

YOU SHOOK ME

This and the following track introduce us to another Bonham speciality: the drama-laden slow blues. 'Shook Me' starts with an exaggeratedly 'dotted' slow shuffle, purposely stiff and mannered in feel. It's excruciatingly held back, a ruse Bonzo revelled in at the time. The track reaches a climax at 4.20 with a short stop-time passage and two monumental fills. Both are wholly typical Bonham and delivered at lightning speed. The first involves 32nds between hands (H) and feet (F) – HHFF, HHFF, etc – and the second, even more daring, alternating 32nds (HF, HF etc).

What makes the fills so striking is Bonzo's sound, coupled with the fact that it was unusual at the time to incorporate the bass drum on an equal basis with the hands in rock drum fills. Although Ginger Baker was a major inspiration for this type of pattern, he saved them mostly for his solo, 'Toad'. Bonham incorporated these rumbling, heavy fills into almost every song, and thus heralded drumming's transformation from heavy rock/blues to a brand new form – heavy metal.

DAZED AND CONFUSED

'Dazed' carries on in a similar tempo, but this time Bonzo starts out with a much smoother groove by playing the in-between hi-hat notes linking Jones' legato walking bass. After a minute or so Bonham plays a couple of fills which recall two of his most celebrated predecessors: at 1.24 there's an even-triplet fill reminiscent of Ginger Baker, and immediately afterwards a staccato eighth-note fill which recalls Mitch Mitchell on Hendrix's 'Manic Depression'. It's almost as though Bonzo is announcing his arrival as the crowning figure in the great rock revolution.

Around 2.05 the band dramatically change pace and drop the dynamic into a call-and-response jam where – in particular – Bonzo and Jones swap licks. Here Bonham shows he can play with a light touch, and what's more it's noticeable just how musical his toms sound – they're just as good soft as they are loud.

Bonham certainly wrote the book on solid, brutally direct stadium drumming, but it's ridiculous to say he didn't utilise extreme dynamics. Here on 'Dazed And Confused' is the ultimate proof.

At 2.30 Bonzo counts off a brisk four on the hi-hat and the band rocks out with a guitar solo over Jones' driving bass. Towards the end of this passage – from 4.48 to 4.57 – Bonzo transforms the straight eighth feel into a (triplet feel) rock boogie before launching into a massive four-bar fill, again involving triplets between hands and feet. This type of fill would become synonymous in drummer's minds with Bonzo. To reiterate: it's not so much the pattern that's unusual, it's the sheer power of the execution coupled with the massive sound. As with all great musicians, you hear this and you know immediately who it is. 'Dazed And Confused' developed into one of Zeppelin's live marathons and (despite the band's reservations) the hugely extended version on *The Song Remains The Same* is still stupendous, dramatic and takes your breath away. The slow blues lends itself perfectly to exaggerated dynamics, pregnant pauses and wildly incendiary guitar solos.

You could argue that Zeppelin's approach is more melodramatic than dramatic, that the over-the-top treatment becomes a parody of the yearning emotion of the real blues. As such this would of course appeal to the relative immaturity of the group's young male fans. There's almost a comic-book unreality in their performances. But then again, this was showbiz and this was the world's greatest live rock attraction. Whatever your view, the format appealed hugely to Bonham's sense of the dramatic and dynamic, and allowed him to stamp his huge personality on the track.

COMMUNICATION BREAKDOWN

This early crowd-pleaser again reveals the band bridging the gap between rock and HM. Bonzo's furious three-in-a row eighth-note bass drum figures push the track and take the drumming above the ordinary. Taken at punk speed and intensity, it's certainly not easy to maintain this pattern. Probably the next important drummer to manage it convincingly would be the post-punk Stewart Copeland in the Police, though of course his sound was very different.

On the bootleg Paris TV rehearsal of 'Communication Breakdown' from 1969 there's great footage of the young, slim and fit Bonzo, hair flailing as he tears into his kit. When the band change pace Bonzo plays a gigantic thrashing break using his left hand and right foot while twirling his right stick. This is fabulous stuff from a man determined to be noticed. And what a blast to see a very young Jason doing exactly the same twirling move on his mini-kit a few years later in *The Song Remains The Same* movie (now on video).

HOW MANY MORE TIMES

This mega-jam sees the band working through all sorts of stylistic changes. On drums, it starts with a jazz ride cymbal and soon transforms into the more familiar blues shuffle.

After three minutes it turns into a bolero, which builds to a climax with Jones's descending bass guitar run leading to a dead stop. Bonzo then starts to assert himself with tom tom figures weaving around the guitar and vocal, getting bigger and wilder until a second huge climax, heralded once more by the descending bass guitar. This leads at 5.54 into another feel altogether – a two-handed snare drum groove with funky flams... and another early indication that Bonzo's range could go way beyond straight-ahead rock.

1969

LED ZEPPELIN II

ATLANTIC 588 198 (US: SD8236)

RELEASED: **OCTOBER 1969**

PRODUCED BY: **JIMMY PAGE**

ENGINEERED BY: **GEORGE CHKIANTZ, CHRIS HUSTON, ANDY JOHNS, EDDIE KRAMER**

RECORDED: **BETWEEN MAY AND AUGUST 1969 AT OLYMPIC, MAYFAIR AND MORGAN STUDIOS, LONDON, ENGLAND; MIRROR STUDIO, LOS ANGELES, CA, US; A&R, ATLANTIC AND JUGGY STUDIOS, NEW YORK, NY, US**

MIXED: **AT A&R STUDIO, NEW YORK, NY, US BY EDDIE KRAMER**

Endless touring had become a way of life for the band but they somehow found time to create **Led Zeppelin II** *within a year of their debut. Page worried that the "insane", fragmented nature of the recording sessions would produce a disjointed album. In fact many people considered it a masterpiece. It sold three million copies within months, turning the band, unexpectedly, into superstars. There was less of the atmosphere of the first record, with more of Zeppelin's hard rock edge on show – this album is credited with establishing heavy metal as a genre – but plenty of contrasting dynamics and ingenious touches to leave rivals, and fans, breathless.*

THE TRACKS

WHOLE LOTTA LOVE
(Page/Plant/Jones/Bonham/Willie Dixon)

running time 5.34

WHAT IS AND WHAT SHOULD NEVER BE
(Page/Plant)

4.44

THE LEMON SONG
(Page/Plant/Jones/Bonham/Chester Burnett)

6.19

THANK YOU
(Page/Plant)

4.47

HEARTBREAKER
(Page/Plant/Jones/Bonham)

4.14

LIVIN' LOVING MAID (SHE'S JUST A WOMAN)
(Page/Plant)

2.39

RAMBLE ON
(Page/Plant)

4.23

MOBY DICK
(Page/Jones/Bonham)

4.21

BRING IT ON HOME
(Page/Plant)

4.20

WHOLE LOTTA LOVE

We're so familiar with this riff now we forget that Bonzo could easily have played a simple doubled-up rock'n'roll backbeat. Instead he plays it funky by placing the first backbeat on (slow count) two and delaying the second backbeat till the 'and' of four, thereby creating a rollover effect worthy of early-1970s heroes Little Feat. So although the guitar riff might have inspired a thousand heavy rockers, the drum groove is much closer to a New Orleans second-line groove.

Throughout Bonzo's work there is a keen awareness of soul and funk styles which Zeppelin's later imitators often ignored, or perhaps were simply unaware of. Because Bonzo got a massive sound and could out-rock the greatest, it's easy to miss the subtlety in his grooves. But as we'll see, he came up with any number of not-so-obvious solutions to the great riffs the band presented him with.

From 1.25 the band take a left turn, descending suddenly into a psychedelic nightmarish trance. As Bonzo pedals hard on his hi-hat you can hear the mechanism squeaking under the weight, and the sound of the up-strokes, together with heavy reverb, transform the beat into a rolling eighth-note feel.

Slow congas and speedy bongos create an exotic back-cloth as Bonham tings and pings on his cymbal bells in a passage that, for me, always presages Pink Floyd's 'clocks' interlude on *Dark Side Of The Moon*.

At 4.28 Bonzo leads the band back in with his

most famous minimalist fill with some starkly brutal eighth-notes on the snare. Again it's the unfeasibly fat sound of his snare which allows him to play such a seemingly banal fill and make it sound fantastic. Frank Beard of ZZ Top would later exploit the idea to great effect on hits like 'Gimme All Your Lovin'.

Note, however, that Bonzo's 'straight' eighths, like Ginger Baker's, always have a hint of a swing. They are not perfectly even – something which, incidentally, would confound MIDI song-file programmers in the 1990s.

WHAT IS AND WHAT SHOULD NEVER BE / THE LEMON SONG

On these two tracks Bonham makes effective early use of gongs. They are heard around 3.37 on 'What Is' and at the start of 'Lemon Song'. Coming out of the psychedelic era, Bonzo always included percussion on live concerts, including a gong and congas, later replaced by timpani.

Meanwhile on the drum kit, towards the end of 'The Lemon Song', at 5.24, there's a stunning single-bar fill which consists of 32 mammy-daddy beats played between hands and feet (HHFF etc).

HEARTBREAKER

This medium-tempo throwaway number has a neat, catchy, spiralling riff which Bonzo holds together unremarkably, till around 2.00 when he plays an unbelievable stream of bass-drum 16th notes (HFFF, HFFF) over four bars, leading up to the dead stop and guitar solo. These are easy to miss as, for once, his bass drum is not recorded well.

MOBY DICK

This short version of Bonham's drum-solo piece is disappointing, a curious insert into the rather workaday riff. As stated earlier in the book, this could be largely explained by the fact that it wasn't played as a live solo, but pieced together by Page from tapes of Bonzo jamming in the studio.

Perhaps because Bonham was such a great band drummer, coming up with consistently inventive parts, his solos often seemed musically less satisfying, though a spectacular highlight of live shows. In particular, the examples captured officially on record and film rarely live up to expectations.

Bonzo tried to play something different each time, keeping up the interest by playing with his bare hands (a technique he'd been developing from his mid-teens or younger), with percussion and, later, with electronic effects. Yet even though he claimed to have a set structure in mind for his solos, they rarely came across that way, possibly due to their great length.

There is a bootleg out-take of 'Moby Dick' (brought to my attention by Vital Information drummer Steve Smith) where Bonzo begins his solo with a direct and unmistakable quote from Max Roach's seminal solo piece 'The Drum Also Waltzes'. This is a solid affirmation of Bonham's early awareness of the jazz greats. In the bare-hands section he also uses licks from Joe Morello's 'Castilian Drums' solo from Dave Brubeck's 1963 *Live At Carnegie Hall* concert. Dave Mattacks remembers that Bonzo was also aware of Chico Hamilton's melodic drumming.

During the later sections of the solo there are hand-and-feet combinations which appear in Ginger Baker's 'Toad', and which every late-1960s rock drummer would try to emulate.

But no one played those thunderous snare/tom/bass drum combinations better than John Bonham.

1970

LED ZEPPELIN III

ATLANTIC DELUXE 2401 002 (US: SD7201)

RELEASED: **OCTOBER 1970**

PRODUCED BY: **JIMMY PAGE**

ENGINEERED BY: **ANDY JOHNS**

RECORDED: **1970 AT HEADLEY GRANGE, HAMPSHIRE, ENGLAND WITH ROLLING STONES MOBILE, AND AT ISLAND AND OLYMPIC STUDIOS, LONDON, ENGLAND**

MIXED: **AT ISLAND STUDIO, LONDON, ENGLAND BY ANDY JOHNS, AND ELECTRIC LADY STUDIO, NEW YORK, NY, US BY EDDIE KRAMER**

Led Zeppelin III *marked the dawn of the band's 'folky'*
period. Exhausted from their hectic schedule, Page and
Plant took some time off in rural Wales to recharge,
writing some acoustic-inspired songs while there. When it
came to recording the third album, they were keen to
experiment with different instruments and new sounds –
and their previous success gave them the confidence to do
so. Their live gigs began making a feature of an
'acoustic set' (and Page took to wearing his 'yokel' hat).
They wanted to show what a multi-faceted band they
could be – but the response was mixed. LZIII sold well,
but less than LZII, and was too 'lightweight' (relatively
speaking) for some critics. Even so, there's still plenty of
heads-down, grooving rock'n'roll here. A band with John
Bonham in it was never going to be a folk band.

THE TRACKS

IMMIGRANT SONG
(Page/Plant)

running time 2.23

FRIENDS
(Page/Plant)

3.54

CELEBRATION DAY
(Page/Plant/Jones)

3.28

SINCE I'VE BEEN LOVING YOU
(Page/Plant/Jones)

7.24

OUT ON THE TILES
(Page/Plant/Bonham)

4.05

GALLOWS POLE
(traditional)

4.56

TANGERINE
(Page)

2.57

THAT'S THE WAY
(Page/Plant)

5.37

BRON-Y-AUR STOMP
(Page/Plant/Jones)

4.16

HATS OFF TO (ROY) HARPER
(traditional)

3.42

IMMIGRANT SONG

The album roars off with this great, driving
performance from Bonzo and the band. The
drums are insistent throughout, sticking close to
the syncopated guitar/bass riff. Bonzo had an
uncanny knack of knowing how best to
complement a riff, when to contrast with it and
when to shadow it, as he does here.

CELEBRATION DAY

Here Bonham plays a relatively straightforward
eighth-note rock beat behind the almost
Creedence Clearwater-like guitar riff. At 1.45 there
is a nice up-beat bass drum figure that is typical
Bonham. At 1.52 there is a brief 16th-note snare
drum fill which incorporates flams – tricky to pull
off at this speed and volume, and showing
Bonham's awareness of basic snare drum
rudiments. This was a fill he often used.

SINCE I'VE BEEN LOVING YOU

Continuing in the tradition of 'Dazed And
Confused' this song is perhaps the definitive
flourish of that major ace in the Zeppelin pack,

the epic slow blues. It's a more jazzy, relaxed and confident performance than the earlier slow blues tracks on the first album. Bonzo's cool entrance is with a simple tap on the snare drum and straight into smooth hi-hat eighths. Bonham's taste shows in the superbly sparing use of bass drum and snare drum figures. The sound is of course fabulous, with monster snare and kick and great whooshing crashes.

During the opening passages he plays the by-now familiar game of holding back the groove as far as possible without slowing down. Well, actually, he does slow down fractionally, but it's deliberate. The tension is fantastic. This is of course something which would be almost impossible to get away with today in a post-computer age when consistent tempos are ingrained into our sensibility.

Bonham's taste and musicality is also evident in the way he uses a big-band drummer's technique of 'setting up' the guitar riff at each turnaround. For example, at 1.06 and then at 2.21 he plays a delicate little snare drum lick which serves as a cue for the up-beat syncopation of the riff. This is a technique swing-band drummers developed in order to marshal their horn sections and help them keep their phrases and stabs tight. Bonzo intuitively understood the tricks of the master big-band drummers like Buddy Rich.

At 4.52 there is a dead stop, after which there's a brief but superb drop in dynamic level by the whole band – another trademark ploy which made them such an exciting live act. As much as rhythm, dynamic awareness is an essential ingredient in blues and soul, and it was a lesson that Bonzo and company knew better than any other contemporary British band of the 1960s.

At 6.16 Bonham plays a now familiar HFF HFF HFF HFF fill – triplets between hand and feet – but this time it's a group of nine of them. Not so tricky at this speed, but nicely executed.

OUT ON THE TILES

This track, which was inspired by the drummer himself, has similar (though not the same) phrasing to 'Good Times Bad Times'. Bonham uses a favourite funk groove, in the style of the great soul/R&B drummer Bernard Purdie, which involves playing paradiddle-derived combinations between snare drum and foot (FHFFHF – sing 'paradiddle-diddle'). It's played in exuberant fashion, and although the feel seems to be straight eighths there is in fact a swing. From early on (0.11) Bonzo throws in a neat fill – a triplet between snare and foot. On the outro (3.52) he uses the same fill as the previous track (HFF-HFF), but here the tempo's much faster.

GALLOWS POLE

On this folksy ballad you might expect a more traditional beat, but Bonham, taking his cue from the driving guitars, butts in at 2.04 with the snare drum on all four beats of the bar and the bass drum in-between. This Tamla Motown-style groove really makes the track fly, toughening it up considerably. Towards the end he starts to break up the beat and gets funky with his bass drum again, at one point (4.23) throwing in 'mammy-daddy' fills, HH-FF-HH-FF, in brisk 16th notes.

1971

(UNTITLED) "LED ZEPPELIN IV"

ATLANTIC DELUXE 2401 012 (US: SD7208)

RELEASED: **NOVEMBER 1971**

PRODUCED BY: **JIMMY PAGE**

ENGINEERED BY: **ANDY JOHNS.**

RECORDED: **1971 AT HEADLEY GRANGE, HAMPSHIRE, ENGLAND WITH ROLLING STONES MOBILE, AND OLYMPIC AND ISLAND STUDIOS, LONDON, ENGLAND**

MIXED: **AT OLYMPIC AND ISLAND STUDIOS, LONDON, ENGLAND, BY ANDY JOHNS, GEORGE CHKIANTZ, AND AT SUNSET SOUNDS, LOS ANGELES, CA, US, BY ANDY JOHNS**

VOCAL ON 'THE BATTLE OF EVERMORE': **SANDY DENNY**

*Keeping up the punishing timetable of an album per year, the enigmatically nameless fourth release (commonly referred to as either **Led Zeppelin IV** or 'Four Symbols') introduced the music world to several legendary Zep tracks, as well as an apparent embracing of all things mystical. (Bonham's "symbol" is the three interlocking rings, by the way – which coincidentally also appeared on some beer bottle labels.) It was largely recorded at the rambling, run-down country mansion Headley Grange, where the band often rehearsed and even lived for short periods (until it got too scary for everyone but Page). The building's formidable natural acoustics and spooky atmosphere contributed enormously to the sound of the album. Recording ended in February 1971, but mixing problems meant it wasn't released until November, leading to ill-founded rumours that the band had split. Not likely. Bonzo felt this was their best album so far, saying: "We had so many great ideas..."*

THE TRACKS

BLACK DOG
(Page/Plant/Jones)

running time 4.54

ROCK AND ROLL
(Page/Plant/Jones/Bonham)

3.40

THE BATTLE OF EVERMORE
(Page/Plant)

5.51

STAIRWAY TO HEAVEN
(Page/Plant)

8.00

MISTY MOUNTAIN HOP
(Page/Plant/Jones)

4.38

FOUR STICKS
(Page/Plant)

4.44

GOING TO CALIFORNIA
(Page/Plant)

3.31

WHEN THE LEVEE BREAKS
(Page/Plant/Jones/Bonham/Memphis Minnie)

7.07

BLACK DOG

On this track Zeppelin cemented their penchant for tunes which are a bugger to count. In fact this is the hardest of their work to decipher rhythmically, certainly during the erratic verses of the recorded version. You can start by counting an extra beat, making five, at the end of each instrumental riff following Plant's vocal refrains ... but after that you're on your own.

In fact the middle sections appear stranger than the verses on first hearing, but they actually remain in common time – they're just heavily syncopated. And in a way this underlines the point that, despite all the rhythmic trickery, the feeling you get from 'Black Dog' is a million miles from the 'muso' puzzles of progressive rock. You sense this is how it came about naturally. Any number of bands have written laboriously self-conscious riffs in odd time signatures. But Zeppelin did it because it was fun, the natural thing for capable musicians in an era where experiment and discovery were still welcomed by press and public alike.

Of course, there is a muso streak in the band – Page and Jones being ex-session musicians, Bonzo a genius with a playful nature, and Plant always willing to dive in with improvised vocals. But this is the honest joy of music-making by young guys who could actually play a bit (and which punk – unwittingly, or is it dim-wittingly? – would kill off).

Zeppelin would quite often include an odd-time bar, usually tagged on to the end of a riff or turnaround. (For instance, 'Heartbreaker' on *II* added a beat at 0.48, while 'Out On The Tiles' from *III* dropped one at 0.25.)

Their rhythmic games often came out of the naturally-inspired need to extend or shorten a phrase here and there, an organic process which is found in all heartfelt music, from the delta blues to Stravinsky, and which depends on musical taste, emotion and general inventiveness.

ROCK AND ROLL

Bonzo's great intro here – so simple and yet so distinctive – harks back to the days of early rock'n'roll. Both hands shuffle in unison eighths on snare and half-open hi-hat, accenting a rock 'clave'. Two-handed shuffles were a staple of early boogie, swing and blues drummers, the forerunners of rock percussionists. Apparently Bonham was fooling around with Little Richard's 'You Keep A Knockin'.

There follows a joyous celebration of rock'n'roll, a priceless Zeppelin jam which rivals the best rock ever produced. At the very end an elated Bonzo goes for the big 'stage' ending, one of those muther-of-all-fills where drummers so often come horribly unstuck. Bonham just about pulls it off, though it's not as clean as it might have been. He would do it better on numerous other occasions, and it's great that a couple have been visually recorded for posterity on *The Song Remains The Same* – at the end of 'Rock And Roll' and more particularly 'Dazed And Confused'. It's only when you *see* him do it you appreciate the power. (Also check the end of 'I Can't Quit You Baby' on *Coda*.)

STAIRWAY TO HEAVEN

From the delicate opening it's impossible to imagine how the band will build this definitive piece into a loud and brash climax, and yet it all unfolds naturally, ascending slowly, confidently and ominously throughout.

Bonham doesn't even enter until after four minutes, and then he patiently continues to build the song until, during the guitar solo at 6.23, he unleashes one of his earthquake fills. At the end of the guitar solo at 6.42 he plays just the right flammed snare drum phrase to re-introduce the vocal, by now at full tilt. At the end of this section the drums mirror what's going on in the arrangement. And by the time Bonzo phrases his snare drum precisely along with the guitar – from 7.16, in-between the vocal phrases – it's so inevitable, it's rock perfection. You can't help but be moved by the palpable sense of excitement at reaching such a logical climax.

Deep Purple's Ian Paice has made the point: "I think the legacy John left is the ability to play the simplest parts and patterns with such a powerful and loose but not sloppy feel, and to inherently know when the song had to 'beef up' and hit the roof." Paice's testimony could apply to many Zeppelin tunes, but nowhere better than here.

FOUR STICKS

One of the most unusual tracks from a drumming perspective – an oddity really – and it's very difficult to make out just what Bonzo is doing. He uses four sticks, like a mallet percussion player, and seems to click the rims of his drums while playing continuous rolling tom toms, keeping everything together by pedalling fours on his hi-hat. You could say this is Bonham's precursor to

Steve Gadd's famous four-sticks Latin groove on Paul Simon's 'Late In The Evening'. Playing with four sticks precludes Bonham from hitting as hard as he normally does and this, along with the heavy compression, gives the tom toms a sort of wave-like rippling 'plastic bucket' sound which is both hypnotic and attractive. It's a sound quite unlike any other Zeppelin drum track.

WHEN THE LEVEE BREAKS

This is the Bonzo drum riff that has been sampled time and again, and it's easy to see why. The beat is relatively simple, but the use of the bass drum syncopated on the last 16th of the beat (the 'a' of 2e&a) gives it a funky edge. As so often with Bonzo's grooves, though, it veers slightly towards a triplet feel. So although the beat is undeniably heavy it also swings, making it an ideal bedrock for the loping hip-hop grooves of the sampling generation. The beat is also isolated at the start of the track, which is of course necessary for clean sampling, and the single-bar pattern found its way on to every breakbeat collection in the late 1980s.

Of course, as with all Bonham's work, the pattern only becomes great in conjunction with the sound. The story of the recording of the track in Headley Grange is well-known, with the kit set up on the stone floor at the foot of the massive stairwell, and just a stereo pair of microphones placed on the second landing. Page and Bonham knew exactly what they were after, and fully deserve the acclaim the experiment has brought them.

Bonzo's kit is of course tuned exactly for the occasion and the beat is wide open and laidback, allowing maximum space to savour the resonance of the environment. The cymbals explode in a way they simply never do when recorded in a controlled,

damped room. Bonzo's drums had always sounded great, but now we're talking hammer-of-the-gods. The phrase 'demolishing a shed' was probably invented for this track.

In 1999 *Rhythm* magazine readers voted this the "greatest groove of all time". That's perhaps an exaggeration, but it's testament, 30 years on, that young drummers could still appreciate the musicality, intensity and attitude of this ground-breaking moment in drumming history. Scary.

MISTY MOUNTAIN HOP

This hippy-trippy song could almost be a single. There's a hint of The Small Faces turned HM. The lumbering, insistently simple riff is matched by Bonham's up-front drumming, and together they push the tune along.

There are some great 16th-note fills over the snare and toms at the end of each eight-bar bridge/chorus, for instance at 1.46 and 2.37. Yet again it's Bonzo's monster sound rather than what he plays that is so remarkable and creates such a buzz. Then, as the song reaches the end of its final chorus, in bar eight (3.56) Bonham starts his fill as usual but carries on for a couple of extra bars. The by-now three-bar fill feels almost like a mini drum solo going on underneath the song. It's also much more adventurous than his earlier fills, starting with a fast triplet roll on the snare drum which gears up and unravels over seven beats before opening out across the kit.

Heard today, this kind of fill is a relic of a bygone era when it was still possible to take huge risks and extemporise off-the-wall fills on major rock records. Now, such seemingly indulgent flashiness would frighten most producers to death.

Those were the days ... weren't they?

1973

HOUSES OF THE HOLY
ATLANTIC K50014 (US: SD7255)

RELEASED: **MARCH 1973**

PRODUCED BY: **JIMMY PAGE**

ENGINEERED BY: **EDDIE KRAMER, ANDY JOHNS**

RECORDED: **MAY 1972 AT OLYMPIC AND ISLAND STUDIOS, LONDON, ENGLAND, AND AT STARGROVES, BERKSHIRE, ENGLAND WITH ROLLING STONES MOBILE**

MIXED: **AT OLYMPIC STUDIO, LONDON, ENGLAND, BY KEITH HARWOOD OR ANDY JOHNS; AND AT ELECTRIC LADY STUDIO, NEW YORK, NY, US BY EDDIE KRAMER**

Houses Of The Holy *was the first Zeppelin album to be allowed a 'proper' title, although casual observers might remember it best as 'the one with the naked girls clambering over the rocks on the cover'. Musically it's perhaps one of their weakest collections – its audacious toying with tempos and musical styles certainly confused the hell out of many critics – though it still got to number 1 in the album charts in both Britain and America. By turns dreamy, exotic, quirky and playful, it was undoubtedly Led Zeppelin's most unpredictable album to date – and not necessarily in a way everyone appreciated. Strangely – but suitably inscrutably – the actual track 'Houses Of The Holy', which was originally recorded for this album in 1972, didn't surface till 1975's Physical Graffiti.*

THE TRACKS

THE SONG REMAINS THE SAME
(Page/Plant)

running time 5.28

THE RAIN SONG
(Page/Plant)

7.39

OVER THE HILLS AND FAR AWAY
(Page/Plant)

4.47

THE CRUNGE
(Page/Plant/Jones/Bonham)

3.13

DANCING DAYS
(Page/Plant)

3.41

D'YER MAK'ER
(Page/Plant/Jones/Bonham)

4.22

NO QUARTER
(Page/Plant/Jones)

6.59

THE OCEAN
(Page/Plant/Jones/Bonham)

4.30

THE SONG REMAINS THE SAME

The long intro has a similar flavour to the overture for The Who's *Tommy*, and it's tempting to make a comparison with Keith Moon. Bonham plays it rather tighter, utilising half-opened hi-hats where Moon would probably have gone for an all-out ride cymbal thrash.

Also, whereas Moon was up and down, Bonham stays solidly in control, moving inexorably towards the climax. Which is not to say that he was metronomically perfect all the time...

Ian Paice makes the general observation that Bonham would not have liked click tracks at all. "You can hear in his playing that he felt, as I do, that within the limitations of the tempo, middle-eights push and verses pull."

THE RAIN SONG

On this amazing orchestrated ballad Bonham waits till 3.37 and then comes in with restrained and tasteful *brushes*. As the arrangement explodes in time-honoured Zeppelin fashion at 5.02 he stays with the brushes, although it's easy to think he's changed to sticks. It's quite possible to get a loud sound from brushes by playing harder and striking with the lowest part of the brush, where the strands are rooted into the stem handle. Around the 7.00 mark Bonzo drops right down, and eventually out, demonstrating once more his excellent dynamic control.

OVER THE HILLS AND FAR AWAY

Bonham again does something a little unusual here. While following Page's riff, as he so often does, he strikes the open hi-hat and closes it on the next beat to get a 'shoop' sound. Yet somehow he manages to keep it open a fraction longer than most drummers would, so the note length overhangs the short guitar note. Yet again, in this attention to detail, Bonzo shows his musicality by extracting the maximum effect from an everyday drumming technique.

THE CRUNGE

Zeppelin in playful mood, and glorying in their virtuosity. Here Bonzo demonstrates how he could perfectly easily have gone the fusion route and 'done a Brand X' like Phil Collins. The track obviously owes a lot to Bonzo, starting with, and going out on a circular 9/8 drum pattern which Bonzo has obviously been working on. In-between he plays syncopated funky riffs with what would be heavy-handed vigour by anyone else. But since it's Bonzo the whole thing somehow grooves along infectiously, delighting in its own lop-sidedness.

The track gradually reveals itself as a homage to James Brown's exhortation to "take me to the bridge" from 'Sex Machine' (1970). And it works, even though Bonzo approaches the drums in an up-front manner, whereas the aim of Brown's drummers was to snuck effortlessly inside the groove. But then Brown's didn't deal so much in odd time signatures as in beautiful syncopation.

D'YER MAK'ER

By contrast, Zeppelin next have a go at reggae. Oh dear. I do believe this is the one track where Bonham comes unstuck (again, we heard an explanation earlier in the book, when John Paul Jones stated that Bonzo just didn't like playing reggae, claiming it was 'boring'). The groove here is post-Sly Dunbar funk-rock reggae and the fills are close to what a reggae drummer might play, but on this occasion it is Bonham's sound – of all things – that lets him down. The problem is that most 1970s reggae was recorded on heavily-damped kits, very often on single-headed toms covered in tape – the very opposite of Bonham's philosophy. For once the genre clash is too great and Bonzo sounds like he really *is* demolishing a shed, and not very tidily. Sorry, guys.

THE OCEAN

Just for the record, the opening section has an eighth-note lopped off each second bar, effectively making this a riff in 17/8. Very 'progressive' rock! But no matter, the result is still a big, meaty, funky Zeppelin blast.

1975

PHYSICAL GRAFFITI

SWAN SONG SSK89400 (US: SS2200)

RELEASED: **FEBRUARY 1975**

PRODUCED BY: **JIMMY PAGE**

ENGINEERED BY: **GEORGE CHKIANTZ, KEITH HARWOOD, ANDY JOHNS, EDDIE KRAMER, RON NEVISON**

RECORDED: **BETWEEN 1970 AND 1974 AT HEADLEY GRANGE, HAMPSHIRE, ENGLAND WITH ROLLING STONES MOBILE AND RONNIE LANE'S MOBILE, AND AT OLYMPIC AND ISLAND STUDIOS, LONDON, ENGLAND**

MIXED: **AT OLYMPIC STUDIO, LONDON, ENGLAND BY KEITH HARWOOD AND AT ELECTRIC LADY STUDIO, NEW YORK, NY, US BY EDDIE KRAMER**

After a gap of two years (abnormally long by Led Zeppelin's standards, negligible by today's) the classic double-album **Physical Graffiti** *silenced the rumour-mongers and sceptics. In fact there had been set-backs – Jones had left the band temporarily in 1974, Plant had throat problems – and Zeppelin hadn't toured for over a year, so their profile was unusually low. But Graffiti brought them back with a bang, and their legendary gigs at Earl's Court cemented their status as rock gods. Their sixth album was a bold return to form, bristling with self-belief and aplomb, if overlong, as most double-albums are – padded slightly with stuff left from earlier projects. It included some of their most musically complex tracks, alongside top-flight down and dirty groove-driven rock. No one knew at the time, but Zep had just peaked. They'd never be this joyful or convincing again.*

THE TRACKS

CUSTARD PIE

(Page/Plant)

running time 4.13

THE ROVER

(Page/Plant)

5.36

IN MY TIME OF DYING

(Page/Plant/Jones/Bonham)

11.04

HOUSES OF THE HOLY

(Page/Plant)

4.01

TRAMPLED UNDERFOOT

(Page/Plant/Jones)

5.35

KASHMIR

(Page/Plant/Bonham)

8.31

IN THE LIGHT

(Page/Plant/Jones)

8.44

BRON-YR-AUR

(Page)

2.06

DOWN BY THE SEASIDE

(Page/Plant)

5.14

TEN YEARS GONE

(Page/Plant)

6.31

NIGHT FLIGHT

(Page/Plant/Jones)

3.36

THE WANTON SONG

(Page/Plant)

4.06

BOOGIE WITH STU

(Page/Plant/Jones/Bonham/Ian Stewart/Mrs Valens)

3.51

BLACK COUNTRY WOMAN

(Page/Plant)

4.24

SICK AGAIN

(Page/Plant)

4.43

CUSTARD PIE

As ever, the album starts with a solid up-front Bonham stormer, this time a heavy rock Bo Diddley groove, played by Bonzo in a tight but still rocking fashion. The title could be read as a slap-in-the-face to the doubters during Zep's lay-off. Bonzo's sure-fisted hi-hat 16ths – with a strong eighth-note emphasis – keep everything motoring along nicely throughout the entire track.

IN MY TIME OF DYING

This traditional song develops into a marathon 11-minute bluesy jam. As Plant sings at one point, "Feels pretty good up here." Bonham kicks in with an on-beat pattern made interesting by use of 16th-note bass drum figures again. Then at 3.50, as the pace and mood pick up, Bonham shifts gear, unleashing one of his most inventive and exciting rhythms. As so often before it's structured closely around the guitar riff, but it's the way he orchestrates it on the kit which is so great. Because his bass drum control is so adept he can toss in a couple of extra beats that most rock drummers would not attempt. His drumming is more akin here to the shattering fusion style emerging at this time, led by the likes of Billy Cobham, Lenny White and Alphonse Mouzon.

After five minutes the track picks up even more and takes off into a slick guitar solo, the furious bass drum now working overtime beneath a 16th-note hi-hat. The sense of danger is underlined by the occasional (very slight) slip, at 5.45 for instance. Nowadays of course this sort of minuscule human glitch would be 'repaired'. In fact the whole track, an adventurous and exploratory studio jam, would today probably be edited to half this length. Whether that's good or bad I'll leave you to decide.

This section ends with great unison figures when the cymbals simply explode and the monumental drum sound threatens to overload the speakers.

HOUSES OF THE HOLY

Bonham chooses to play relatively straight through this optimistic and catchy riff, pushing and stoking the band along with a relaxed confidence. At 1.43 (and again at 2.47) there's a delightful, slightly cookie touch where he plays 16ths between hi-hat and very light 'ghosted' snare strokes. The effect is to make the band 'float' for a moment. Love it.

TRAMPLED UNDERFOOT

A Stevie Wonder-style clavinet groove bounds through this funky dance piece. In fact the racing keyboard and guitar riffs occasionally seem to speed up and slow down around the central anchoring drums. It's a strange, unsettling effect which again would probably not survive today. This is exactly the sort of track that would be sequenced together to sound rhythmically perfect and mechanical. The way Zeppelin play it is anything but mechanical.

There are some great triplet rolls on the turnarounds, for instance at 3.05. And at 5.05 Bonzo throws in a string of hi-hat 'barks' in a new place for him – exactly one 16th before and after the fourth beat of each bar. This is a trick that funk drummers learned in the mid 1970s, and again Bonham shows he was aware of what the late Tony Williams would have called "hip drum shit".

KASHMIR

This piece – with its riffs like shifting sands continually weaving around the immovable drumming of John Bonham – is considered by many to be Zeppelin's finest work. As the music became more sophisticated Bonham increasingly found the maturity and confidence to seek out the cleanest, most direct way of expression. It may not be so much fun for the drummers in the audience, but on Zeppelin's most majestic songs Bonham was happy to play uncluttered beats which could be heard and understood by the massive crowds – and, as on 'Kashmir', which unified the broad canvas of the music. This sensibility was rarer in Bonzo's day than now.

1976

PRESENCE

SWAN SONG SSK59402 (US: SS8416)

RELEASED: **MARCH 1976**

PRODUCED BY: **JIMMY PAGE**

ENGINEERED BY: **KEITH HARWOOD**

RECORDED: **DURING NOVEMBER AND DECEMBER 1975 AT MUSICLAND STUDIO, MUNICH, WEST GERMANY**

MIXED: **MUSICLAND STUDIO, MUNICH, WEST GERMANY BY KEITH HARWOOD**

Presence had a painful birth. After the highs of 1975 (huge hit album, massive 10th US tour) came the lows, from minor injuries and illnesses to Plant's car crash, which forced another lay-off. It did provide a chance to work on new songs, although perhaps with less vigour and relish than previously. *Presence* was recorded quickly, largely thanks to superhuman efforts by Page, who later called this a "guitar album" – meaning electric guitar – with "no keyboards and no mellowness". A severe, unflinching LP, less adventurous than before, it still threw in a few unexpected twists. Page felt it was "underrated". The soundtrack of the band's movie *The Song Remains The Same* was released five months later and was a rather flat live collection, with no new tracks. Fans had to wait three years for Zeppelin's next original album.

THE TRACKS

ACHILLES LAST STAND
(Page/Plant)

running time 10.22

FOR YOUR LIFE
(Page/Plant)

6.20

ROYAL ORLEANS
(Page/Plant/Jones/Bonham)

2.58

NOBODY'S FAULT BUT MINE
(Page/Plant)

6.27

CANDY STORE ROCK
(Page/Plant)

4.07

HOTS ON FOR NOWHERE
(Page/Plant)

4.43

TEA FOR ONE
(Page/Plant)

9.27

ACHILLES LAST STAND

Presence kicks off with this epic piece in which, following a brief introduction, Bonzo roars in on a full-ahead furious rock beat with typically speedy bass drum slotted between the backbeats. At 1.17 he throws in an amazing Buddy Rich-like triplet roll right around the kit, as impressive as you're ever likely to hear, showing terrific hand control and power. At 2.30 he introduces another new fill, which involves playing consecutive hand-to-hand 16th notes (RLRLR), the first three beats on the snare and the fourth and fifth on the left and right crash cymbals, underpinned by the bass drum. This is a simple but very effective idea that actually became hip with rock drummers in the 1990s.

Towards the end of the track, after all of nine minutes, Bonzo somehow manages to up the intensity of the groove even further by adding a disco-style open hi-hat on the 'and' of each beat. Whatever it takes…

FOR YOUR LIFE

The band start off paying musical homage to their mates, Free, with guitar and bass locked into hard-edged soulful riffs. Bonham holds together the rather dark and spacious groove with a tight hi-hat and tambourine, where Free's drummer Simon Kirke might have gone for a looser forearm-smashing approach.

At 2.07 a new riff emerges which inspires Bonham to slip in a couple of fast triplet beats with his foot. The interesting thing about this is that it becomes – coincidentally I'm sure – a precursor to the type of swing beat popularised in the 1980s by so-called go-go bands like Trouble Funk, who in turn paved the way for the emergence of hip-hop-style grooves.

ROYAL ORLEANS

This tune, part-written by Bonham, starts with the band in unison on a melodic riff, which leads into a funk-rock groove again. And at 0.57 Bonzo appropriates another Purdie-ism – while playing 16th notes hand-to-hand on his hi-hat he nimbly accentuates the first three left-hand up-beats as hi-hat 'barks'. This sort of funk drumming requires total balance and sophisticated four-way co-ordination, accenting the hi-hat with the left hand while quickly lifting the left foot to open and close the cymbals.

To emphasise one more time: for an HM bruiser this man knew his soul/R&B. Perhaps this is the place to quote the comments of Steve Smith, one of the greatest virtuoso drummers working today, who has made a serious study of Bonham's playing (and even recorded an amazing up-tempo 'jazz' homage to 'Moby Dick'). He points out that, apart from his incredible sound, Bonham has a unique balance between his limbs. "It's important to realise his feel has a swing factor to it. He embodied the swing of Gene Krupa and Cozy Cole, the chops of Buddy Rich, some of the ideas from Max Roach and Elvin Jones, and then the funk of the James Brown drummers and Al Jackson. You can hear it all." Well, you couldn't have a greater commendation than that.

CANDY STORE ROCK

Here is rockabilly given a spirited contemporary treatment and coupled with an Elvis/Eddie Cochran-style slap-back echoing vocal. The track bounces along, creating a good-time party vibe, the whole band locked tightly together in a combined assault. The drumming is inspired, with an up-front cymbal bell continually lifting the rhythm and ensuring things don't get too heavy. As the track progresses there's some typically sneaky Zeppelin-style messing with the timing of the alternating riffs as they jolt back and forth, in and out of the picture.

HOTS ON FOR NOWHERE

The band experiment with another ahead-of-its-time feel, this one almost a precursor of acid jazz, with Bonzo playing jazz shuffle/swing over a half-time pulse. Typically, he eats it up. Around 2.50 Bonham doubles up the backbeat into a sort of rockabilly shuffle. It's interesting that so many of Zeppelin's tracks could be played as two-beat rock'n'roll but Bonzo chooses to play half-time, making them funkier, heavier and more authoritative. On the outro, at 4.04, Bonzo pulls off another fill, typical of many he's played before, but because of the triplet shuffle context it becomes almost Steve Gadd-like as he squeezes a lot of awkward, angular beats into a tight space.

TEA FOR ONE

The band return to the old favourite slow blues – but this time there's more of a low-key smoky nightclub atmosphere than previously. Bonzo's kick is exposed between the spacious riff, and you can hear the bass drum's own self-contained reverb, resulting from the cavernous interior of the un-damped drum.

Bonzo revels in playing lots of single-stroke crescendo rolls as the song builds.

1 9 7 9

IN THROUGH THE OUT DOOR

SWAN SONG SSK59410 (US: SS16022)

RELEASED: **AUGUST 1979**

PRODUCED BY: **JIMMY PAGE**

ENGINEERED BY: **LEIF MASES**

RECORDED: **DURING NOVEMBER AND DECEMBER 1978 AT POLAR STUDIOS, STOCKHOLM, SWEDEN**

MIXED: **PLUMPTON STUDIO, ENGLAND**

In Through The Out Door was the last Zeppelin album released during John Bonham's lifetime. It was also their first for three years. 1977 had been disastrous for the band – with the infamous assault charges and shocking death of Plant's son – and it took them two years to recover. But this 'comeback' release was better than anyone could have expected, and more experimental than they'd been for a long time, utilising the new technology at Abba's state-of-the-art studios. The band had thrown themselves back into work with renewed energy (both in the studio and on-stage), and were having more fun than they'd had for ages – though there's a bittersweet quality here, particularly viewed with hindsight. At the time things seemed to be looking up... until Bonzo's deadly vodka binge in September 1980.

THE TRACKS

IN THE EVENING
(Page/Plant/Jones)

running time 6.49

SOUTH BOUND SAUREZ
(Plant/Jones)

4.12

FOOL IN THE RAIN
(Page/Plant/Jones)

6.12

HOT DOG
(Page/Plant)

3.17

CAROUSELAMBRA
(Page/Plant/Jones)

10.32

ALL MY LOVE
(Plant/Jones)

5.53

I'M GONNA CRAWL
(Page/Plant/Jones)

5.30

IN THE EVENING

Following a mysterious atmospheric opening, the band explodes straight in on the 'one'. Bonzo is superbly sparing. Listening to this track you can hear the next generation of supergroups like U2 and Simple Minds: the sparse no-nonsense guitar riff pre-dates U2's Edge, while Bonzo's minimalist drumming would be the blueprint for drummers like Simple Minds' own powerhouse, Mel Gaynor.

With the rapidly advancing recording technology, Bonzo's drums sound better than ever. You can hear the flap of the bass drum head as he strikes off it, plus there's that unmistakable 'crack' – and the only way you can get that is with both drum heads on and next to no damping.

SOUTH BOUND SAUREZ

The band return to a favourite rock'n'roll New Orleans feel, with the drum pattern based on a reverse 'Bo Diddley' 2:3 clave. The snare drum sounds tighter than usual, or perhaps it's just a bit lower in the mix than normal. Further indication that the band was experimenting at this time?

FOOL IN THE RAIN

This is another fascinating performance from Bonham, although it's rarely mentioned. Yet again he opts for a half-time feel with the backbeat on three. What he actually plays is a technically tricky rhythm generally ascribed to the great Bernard Purdie, and known by drummers as a 'Purdie Shuffle'. Funnily enough Purdie's best-known exposition of his shuffle appeared later than

Bonham's, on Steely Dan's 'Babylon Sisters' (1980). And Jeff Porcaro won a Grammy for his version on Toto's hit 'Rosanna' (1983). Bonham was obviously hip to the rhythm years before most drummers had mastered it. What's difficult about the groove is that while the right hand shuffles in normal fashion the left hand plays soft 'ghost' notes in between – RLR RLR RLR – but still has to accent the backbeat on beat three. Meanwhile the bass drum picks out the bass groove.

Bonham makes the rhythm even trickier by opening and closing the hi-hat for a 'shoop' effect on the upbeat triplet of beat one – 1&a. During the bridges Bonham changes the rhythm to a more Afro-Cuban 6/4 vibe with his cymbal bell pattern crossing the groove.

As with so many Zeppelin arrangements there is an unexpected twist when, half-way through, the band double the tempo and roar into a sort of street samba. Bonzo's approach is inevitably a little heavy-handed by purist standards, but he's evidently aware of the caixa (snare drum) rhythms of Brazilian samba schools. The groove is a mish-mash of Brazilian and Cuban/Latin feels, and Bonham climaxes the section with a manic timbale-like triplet snare drum roll which lands right on beat one of the returning original groove.

All this is evidence that Bonham was keeping his ears open and developing his technique all the time. It provides a taster of his capabilities, and an indication of what he might have gone on to do.

CAROUSELAMBRA

With Jones' keyboards leading the way, 'Carouselambra' is Zeppelin's most modern-sounding track – something like Van Halen's 'Jump', but half a decade earlier. Bonham's approach is once more the model for all the stadium drummers who followed him. Towards the end the band even sound like they could be playing in the 1990s.

Was this the way the band might have evolved, or was it too radical, and would they have split or lost their audience anyway? We'll never know.

1982

CODA

SWAN SONG 7900511 (US: 900511)

RELEASED: **NOVEMBER 1982**

PRODUCED BY: **JIMMY PAGE**

ENGINEERED BY: **ANDY JOHNS, LEIF MASES, VIC MAILE, JOHN TIMPERLEY**

RECORDED: **BETWEEN 1970 AND 1978 AT MOUNTAIN STUDIO, MONTREUX, SWITZERLAND; OLYMPIC STUDIO, LONDON, ENGLAND; POLAR STUDIOS, STOCKHOLM, SWEDEN; ROYAL ALBERT HALL, LONDON, ENGLAND WITH PYE MOBILE; SOL STUDIO, COOKHAM, BERKSHIRE, ENGLAND; STARGROVES, BERKSHIRE, ENGLAND WITH ROLLING STONES MOBILE**

MIXED: **SOL STUDIO, COOKHAM, BERKSHIRE, ENGLAND BY STUART EPPS**

*After Bonham's death there would be no new Zeppelin material, but over the subsequent couple of years Jimmy Page pieced together **Coda**, a collection of live recordings and studio out-takes assembled from the band's archives (covering 1970-1978). He also brought in Plant and Jones to add overdubs and flesh out some of the tracks. A must-have for all grieving Zeppelin fans, it still sold a million. Although there was a good cross-section of styles, and some nostalgic delights, there were no great musical revelations on offer. Bonham's electronic odyssey, 'Montreux', was actually started back in 1976, and resurrected here by Page as a posthumous tribute. Many felt that it was a somewhat unusual epitaph, but it undeniably encapsulates Bonzo's consistent desire to avoid doing the obvious thing.*

THE TRACKS

WE'RE GONNA GROOVE

(Ben E King/James Bethea)

running time 2.37

POOR TOM

(Page/Plant)

3.02

I CAN'T QUIT YOU BABY

(Willie Dixon)

4.16

WALTER'S WALK

(Page/Plant)

4.31

OZONE BABY

(Page/Plant)

3.35

DARLENE

(Page/Plant/Jones/Bonham)

4.37

BONZO'S MONTREUX

(Bonham)

4.18

WEARING AND TEARING

(Page/Plant)

5.28

WE'RE GONNA GROOVE / I CAN'T QUIT YOU BABY

Both tracks were recorded at London's Royal Albert Hall in 1970. The former is a funk-blues, where at times the band sound close to the Jimi Hendrix Experience. Bonzo drives the piece with an insistent ride bell pattern and throws in a superbly controlled snare drum obbligato over three bars from 1.46 through to 1.51.

The latter track is actually a soundcheck jam. It's particularly revealing because it shows Bonham deliberately overplaying, trying out his licks almost like warm-up exercises. As with all drummers, Bonham's studio tracks are somewhat subdued in comparison with the wilder live performances, and here he shows some more of his capabilities. There are lovely press rolls leading into the softer dynamics (for example at 0.58). At the finish, as the band drops out, he rehearses one of those big endings which almost amounts to a drum solo. Fantastic stuff, echoing all around the historic concert hall.

POOR TOM

Also from 1970, but this time a studio recording (from Olympic), this piece has Bonzo playing a tasty New Orleans-style rock'n'roll side-drum groove. Brisk eighth-notes are played on the snare instead of the hi-hat while the syncopated bass drum beats lock in tightly beneath.

WALTER'S WALK

From 1972, this is another muscular Bonzo performance. After five seconds he crashes in on the end of the intro guitar riff with his bass drum and snare drum locked together, like a barn door slamming in a gale. It's an almost frighteningly violent sound, as Bonzo drives off into an uptempo rocker with his bass drum working flat out again.

DARLENE

This Bonzo/Jones composition is a basic workaday rocker ... but at 3.28 there is one of those straightforward rolls over the top of the kit, the snare and toms. It's nothing technically complex and yet it sounds incredible, just because of the sound and the delivery.

BONZO'S MONTREUX

Unlike Bonzo's earlier solo feature, 'Moby Dick', 'Montreux' is far more satisfying. On first listening it may not thrill those fans who would have liked to hear a recording of a more typical drum solo, of the virtuoso showing-off kind. But they'd tried that on record and it hadn't worked – Bonzo's solos were best left to the live arena where he excelled. 'Montreux', on the other hand, is tightly structured, like a 'song' for drum kit and overdubbed percussion. Although relatively simple, chops-wise, it's a grower and can be followed by anyone – not just other drummers.

The basis is a pretty straightforward kit groove, solid and devoid of flashy fills. You could be forgiven for thinking Bonzo is playing double bass drums, because his single kick is so powerful and insistent, filling all the gaps between the snare beats. The piece builds as timpani, timbales and other percussion and electronics are gradually added to the mêlée. It's very steady, and Bonzo's timing is noticeably great. The many overdubs all lock together tightly – there was no quantising or digital 'cheating' in those days – and again demonstrate Bonzo's technical control.

WEARING AND TEARING

Recorded in 1978 in Stockholm, this has been described as Zeppelin's answer to punk, though in truth it's all a bit too tight, tuneful and expertly played, too 'musical' for punk. It's closer to a Zeppelin parody of over-the-top mid-1970s glam rock. You could easily imagine The Sweet – no mean rockers themselves in their heyday – releasing this frantic headbanger.

Whichever way you look at it, it's a great blockbuster, and no one's having more of a ball than the drummer. Which is surely the way we should remember Bonzo.

OTHER RECORDINGS

Two further CD collections that contain some interesting work from Bonham are the BBC radio sessions and The Song Remains The Same soundtrack, details of which are given on this page. There are also a number of Zeppelin compilations, some officially remastered in glorious digital sound by Jimmy Page.

BBC SESSIONS

Atlantic 83061 (US: 830612)

Released: October 1997

Produced by: Jimmy Page

Original BBC producers: Bernie Andrews, Jeff Griffin, John Walters

Recorded between March 1969 and April 1971 at BBC Aeolian Hall studio 2, London, England; BBC Maida Vale studio 4, London, England; BBC Paris Cinema, London, England; BBC Playhouse Theatre, London, England. Originally broadcast between March 1969 and April 1971 on Chris Grant's *Tasty Pop Sundae*, *One Night Stand*, *Radio 1 In Concert*, and *Top Gear* BBC radio programmes

You Shook Me (Willie Dixon/JB Lenoir)

I Can't Quit You Baby (Willie Dixon)

Communication Breakdown (Page/Jones/Bonham)

Dazed And Confused (Page)

The Girl I Love She Got Long Black Wavy Hair (Sleepy John Estes)

What Is And What Should Never Be (Page/Plant)

Communication Breakdown (Page/Jones/Bonham)

Travelling Riverside Blues (Robert Johnson)

Whole Lotta Love (Page/Plant/Jones/ Bonham/Willie Dixon)

Somethin' Else (Eddie Cochran)

Communication Breakdown (Page/Jones/Bonham)

I Can't Quit You Baby (Willie Dixon)

You Shook Me (Willie Dixon/JB Lenoir)

How Many More Times (Page/Jones/Bonham)

Immigrant Song (Page/Plant)

Heartbreaker (Page/Plant/Jones/Bonham)

Since I've Been Loving You (Page/Plant/Jones)

Black Dog (Page/Plant/Jones)

Dazed And Confused (Page)

Stairway To Heaven (Page/Plant)

Going To California (Page/Plant)

That's The Way (Page)

Whole Lotta Love Medley (Boogie Chillun' / Fixin' To Die / That's All Right Mama / A Mess Of Blues)

Thank You (Page/Plant)

THE SONG REMAINS THE SAME

Swan Song SSK89402 (US: SS2201)

Released September 1976

Produced by Jimmy Page

Original soundtrack from the film *The Song Remains The Same* recorded on July 27th, 28th and 29th 1973 during three concerts at Madison Square Garden, New York, NY, US. Mixed at Electric Lady studio, New York, NY, US by Eddie Kramer

Rock And Roll (Page/Plant/Jones/Bonham)

Celebration Day (Page/Plant/Jones)

The Song Remains The Same (Page/Plant)

The Rain Song (Page/Plant)

Dazed And Confused (Page)

No Quarter (Page/Plant/Jones)

Stairway To Heaven (Page/Plant)

Moby Dick (Page/Jones/Bonham)

Whole Lotta Love (Page/Plant/Jones/ Bonham/Willie Dixon)

Page numbers in *italics* indicate illustrations. *Titles in italics* are albums. Titles in 'single quotes' are songs.

ACKNOWLEDGEMENTS

The authors would like to extend grateful thanks for the help, support and encouragement of the many people who contributed towards this book and for the heartfelt enthusiasm and affection expressed towards rock's greatest drummer. In particular we offer special thanks to:

Garry Allcock, Carmine Appice, Bev Bevan, Allan Callan, Richard Cole, Glen Colson, Gary Cubitt, Dennis Detheridge, Liberty Devitto, Sally Gauntlet, David Hadley, Bill Harry, Bill Harvey, Bob Henrit, John Paul Jones, Louise King, Simon Kirke, Paul Leim, Dave Mattacks, Robin Melville, Charlie Morgan, Howard Mylett, Jeff Ocheltree, Ian Paice, Dave Pegg, Ernie Petito, Mac Poole, Greg Prevost, Pat Reid, Dave Seville, Jim Simpson, Steve Smith, Dennis Streatfield, Paul Thompson, Baz Ward, and Will Wright for sharing their memories.

PICTURE CREDITS

Photographs were supplied by the following (number indicates page; source in *italics*):

front jacket *J Mayer/Pictorial Press*; **2** *David Redfern/Redferns;* **7** *Chuck Boyd/Redferns;* **13** *Dick Barnatt/Redferns*; **34** below right *Pictorial Press*; **35** main picture *Dick Barnatt/Redferns*; **35** record sleeve *Atlantic*; **36** main picture *Chuck Boyd/Redferns*; **36** below right *Richard Ecclestone*; **37** top left, centre, right *Chuck Boyd/Redferns*; **37** record sleeve *Atlantic*; **38/39** main picture *Robert Ellis/Repfoto*; **40/41** record sleeve *Atlantic*; **41** *Chuck Boyd/Redferns*; **42** left *Chuck Boyd/Redferns*; **42** top *Robert Knight/Redferns*; **42** right *Pictorial Press;* **43** *Chuck Boyd/Redferns*; **44** top left *Dave Ellis/Redferns*; **44** top *T Hanley/Redferns*; **44** centre *Alan Johnson*; **44** record sleeve *Atlantic*; **45** *Robert Ellis/Repfoto*; **46** left *Pictorial Press*; **46** main picture *Robert Ellis/Repfoto*; **46/47** record sleeve *Atlantic*; **47** all pictures *J Mayer/Pictorial Press*; **48/49** all pictures *Chuck Boyd/Redferns*; **50/51** main picture *S Morley/Redferns*; **50** below right *Phillips Fine Art Auctioneers, (London)*; **51** record sleeves *Swan Song*; **52** top left *Van Houten/Pictorial Press*; **52** below left *J Mayer/Pictorial Press*; **52** below right *Pictorial Press*; **52/53** main *J Mayer/Pictorial Press*; **53** below *James Cumpsty*; **54** record sleeve *Swan Song*; **55** record sleeve *Swan Song*; **55** below right *Richie Aaron/Redferns*; **56/57** *Grant Davis/Redferns*; **58** all pictures *Grant Davis/Redferns*; **59** *The Howard Mylett Collection*; **60** left *Pictorial Press*; **60/61** *Mike Prior/Redferns*; **62** top *Van Houten/Pictorial Press*; **62** record sleeves *Swan Song*; **63** record sleeve *Atlantic*; **63** main picture *Robert Ellis/Repfoto*; **65** *Dick Barnatt/Redferns*; **89** *David Redfern/Redferns*; **109** *Richie Aaron/Redferns;* **127** *Chuck Boyd/Redferns*; **143** *Chuck Boyd/Redferns*; **rear jacket** from the top *Chuck Boyd/Redferns*; *Mike Prior/Redferns*; *David Redfern/Redferns*; *Dick Barnatt/Redferns*.

Other illustrated items including advertisements, record sleeves etc came from the collections of Tony Bacon, Chris Welch and Howard Mylett.

Every effort has been made to acknowledge correctly and contact the source and/copyright holder of each picture, and Outline Press Ltd apologises for any unintentional errors or omissions.

BIBLIOGRAPHY

Paul Kendall *Led Zeppelin, A Visual Documentary* (Omnibus Press, 1982)

Dave Lewis *Led Zeppelin, A Celebration* (Omnibus Press, 1991)

Hugo Pinksterboer *The Cymbal Book* (Hal Leonard, 1992)

Chris Welch *Led Zeppelin, Dazed and Confused* (Carlton, 1998)

Chris Welch *Led Zeppelin the Book* (Proteus, 1984)

Periodicals: *Making Music, Melody Maker, Modern Drummer, Rhythm*.